GEOLOGY ROCKS!

50 HANDS-ON ACTIVITIES TO EXPLORE THE EARTH

Cindy Blobaum

**Illustrations by
Michael Kline**

**Winner
of the
Teachers'
Choice
Award**

williamsonbooks™

NASHVILLE, TENNESSEE

Dedication

To Emily, who considers each rock she finds a treasure.

Acknowledgments

I am deeply indebted to my parents, Gary and Jan Sickbert, as well as to Ken Finch and Ed Peterson. Without their years of encouragement to look at, think about, and explain things differently, this book would never have become a reality. My husband, Philip, provided the confidence and "Daddy days" that were essential to getting it all together. And it would never have gotten off the ground without my editor, Vicky Congdon.

ISBN-13: 978-1-885593-29-0
ISBN-10: 1-885593-29-5

Published by Williamson Books
An imprint of Ideals Publications
A Guideposts Company
Nashville, Tennessee
www.idealsbooks.com

Printed and bound in the United States of America

Library of Congress Cataloging-in-Publication Data

Blobaum, Cindy, 1966-
    Geology rocks! : 50 hands-on activities to explore the earth / Cindy
    Blobaum : illustrations by Michael Kline
    p. cm.
    Includes bibliographical references and index.
    Summary: Presents fifty hands-on activities to introduce the science
    of geology and explain the formation and history of the earth.
        (alk. paper)
        1. Geology–Experiments–Juvenile literature.
    [1. Geology–Experiments. 2. Experiments.]
    I. Kline, Michael P., ill. II. Title.
    QE29.B57   1999
    551'.078–dc21   98-53299
                                                CIP
                                                AC

Kaleidoscope Kids® Series Editor: Susan Williamson
Designed by: Joseph Lee Designs: Joseph Lee,
    Kristin DiVona, Sue Yee
Illustrations © 1999 by Michael Kline

Kaleidoscope Kids® is a registered trademark of
Ideals Publications.

Wals_Oct10_8

Photography: page 16: U.S. Dept. of the Interior, U.S. Geological Survey, David A. Johnston Cascades Volcano Observatory, Vancouver, WA, Austin Post (eruption), Daniel Dzurisin (car), Lyn Topinka (mailboxes), David Wieprecht (1990); page 30: Andy Ninowsky/courtesy of Cave Michelangelo; page 42: NASA; page 54: David Weintraub/Photo Researchers, Inc.; page 60: Art Resource; page 20, page 70: Detroit Publishing Company Photograph Collection, Library of Congress Prints and Photographs Division, Washington D.C.; page 71, page 79: Corbis Royalty Free Collection; page 79: U.S. Dept. of the Interior, National Park Service, Glacier National Park; page 78, 87: U.S. Dept. of the Interior National Park Service, Photographic Library.

Contents

Geology? It's Everywhere!

Take a good look around you. From the can that holds your soda to the gas that makes your car go, from your iron-fortified breakfast cereal to the coins in your piggy bank, geology is all *around* you — and *in* you! It affects just about anything you can think of, from your health to where your house is built. It tells you how the water you drink travels to your tap, and where to bury the dead. There's geology at work on the supermarket shelves, in your classroom, in your body — even in many of our common expressions (have you ever been *petrified* while watching a scary movie?).

When you look at the world through the eyes of a geologist, you recognize the secrets hidden in the rock you hold in your hand, and you notice the path a glacier might have taken through your neighborhood. You'll understand the forces that shaped the mountain you're climbing or the beach where you're digging sand castles, and you'll know the best places to look for fossils.

Geology isn't *just* rocks, but for sure, geology rocks!

Earth's Treasure Chest

"If we took all of the earth products out of our lives, we would be hungry, naked, and shivering in the dark."

—Duane L. Leavitt, earth science teacher in Maine

Did you have *cereal* for breakfast in a *ceramic* bowl this morning and drink juice from a *glass*? Brush your teeth with *toothpaste* and fill a *glass* with *water* to rinse? Turn off the *lamp* before you left the room? Stuff your sandwich in a *plastic* bag and grab some *change* for milk money? Pick up a *pencil* to finish last night's homework? Whew! Without even thinking about it, you used, at the very least, 10 geological earth treasures just getting ready for school. (And you thought geology was just about rock collecting!)

We are lucky enough to live on a huge treasure chest full of riches we use every day — it's called planet Earth! We use our geological treasures in so many ways that once you start to think about it, you'll realize the earth is a real mine (and not just full of gold!).

Language Links

The word *geology* — the study of earth and its history — comes to us from Greek. *Ge* means "earth" in Greek, and *logy* (from the Greek word *logos*) means "the study of."

Spot the Treasure

Gather the following items: a thumbtack, a penny, a baking pan, a soda can, a coffee mug, a margarine tub, and a lightbulb.

Look over the items and make a list of what they're made of. Can you name the one thing everything on your list has in common?

Your list probably looks something like this: metal, copper, more metal, aluminum, clay, plastic, glass. All of those materials come from the earth. Some we take right out of the earth, like copper for pennies. Others we make from earth materials, like glass (made from sand).

How many things around the room you're sitting in are made from metal, plastic, or glass? Life would be pretty different without using anything made from these materials, wouldn't it? And you've only peeked into earth's treasure chest. Let's open it further!

THE MINERAL CLUB

Before you bite into an ear of corn, do you sprinkle it with *salt*? Does your little brother or sister play out in the yard in a *sand* box? And can you find some objects around your house made with modeling *clay*? Welcome to the Mineral Club! You might not know the word *mineral*, but you use minerals all the time.

Minerals are a big group of special earth materials. They include everyday items like salt, sand, and clay as well as sparkly jewels like diamonds and rubies. Minerals also occur as useful metals like gold, silver, copper, and iron. We retrieve these minerals by mining, either with hand tools or with dynamite.

These earth materials all look pretty different, don't they? But, as minerals, they all have something in common (page 36).

Chip Mining

Let's see how good you would be as a miner (using hand tools, of course!).

You will need:
- 🍪 A chocolate chip cookie
- 🍪 2 toothpicks

Look carefully at where the chocolate chips are located. Imagine those chips are nuggets of gold you want to remove from the earth (cookie) with your tools (toothpick) to use in your jewelry factory. You'll be paid $500 for each whole chip you get out. To make sure you take good care of the earth, you will have to pay a $100 fine for every broken cookie piece that is larger than a pencil eraser. How much did you earn in the chip mine?

Think About It!

Is There a Better Way?

How did your earth cookie look when you were finished mining? No matter how careful you were, it won't look the same as when you started. The same is true of mining the real earth.

For many years, miners blasted huge holes in the earth. At some mines, all the plants and trees were scraped off the earth's surface to get to the minerals below. This caused a lot of damage, including water pollution and ugly earth scars. And when the mines were empty, they were abandoned for new sites rich with minerals.

Here's the dilemma: We need those minerals, but we also need to protect the earth. What would you and your friends do? Would you choose minerals over earth, or earth over minerals? Or would you do things a little differently?

A RECYCLING REMINDER

While it might seem as if we have an abundance of sand to make glass or metal to make cans, it takes millions of years and the right geological conditions to create these resources. If we keep using these treasures at our present rate, we'll run out for sure!

Chances are, you already recycle glass, plastic, and metal at home and at your school. That's great! Your family and your classmates are setting a good example of stewardship of the earth. Recycling conserves original materials so there will be plenty left for generations of kids after you!

Amazing Aluminum!

Aluminum is one of the most abundant metals on earth. One of the handy things about aluminum is that it can be recycled over and over. What's more, recycling aluminum uses much less energy than mining the mineral bauxite *from the earth to produce new aluminum.*

You choose: You can throw that soda can in the recycling bin, and it can be part of your child's soda can in 20 years and then part of your grandchild's can in another 20 years and then ...

Or you can put your can in the landfill, where it'll still be around about 500 years from now — as trash!

This Water Is as Hard as a Rock!

Fill a glass with water from the faucet and take a close look at it. Do you see any metals floating around? The water you drink might have minerals in it, but you usually can't tell by looking at it. Take a sip. If there were a lot of minerals, your water might have a faint metallic taste. Here's a way to test it for sure.

The next time it rains, put a clean pan outside to collect rainwater. Pour enough rainwater into a clear jar to fill it ³/4 full. Next, fill another clear jar that's the same size ³/4 full with water from the faucet. Add ¹/2 teaspoon (2 ml) of dish detergent to both jars, put on the lids and shake. Compare the amount of soapsuds in the jars.

When water is full of minerals, such as iron, it's called hard water. Soap doesn't make a lot of suds in hard water. Water that doesn't have a lot of minerals in it is called soft water, and it will turn sudsy. Which water is softer?

Mad as a Hatter!

In the 1860s when Abraham Lincoln was president of the United States, people liked to wear hats made out of beaver skins, because Lincoln did. To get most of the fur off the skin, hatters (the people who made the hats) soaked the skins in the mineral *mercury* (the same mineral that is inside a thermometer).

What they didn't know then is that mercury is poisonous to people. It soaked into the hatters' blood through their skin, and eventually the poison started affecting their brains. The hatters would make weird faces, walk funny, mumble to themselves, and do other strange things. People started using the expression "mad as a hatter" to describe someone who acted in an odd or peculiar way. But the hatters weren't mentally ill — they were suffering from mercury poisoning.

Read Those Labels!

Grab a box of your favorite breakfast cereal. On it, you'll see all sorts of nutrition information about vitamins and — yes — minerals! Do you see the mineral calcium *on there? How about* sodium *(common salt)? Some minerals, like iron, calcium, and sodium, are so important that you could get sick if you didn't have them. (But other minerals, like mercury, are poisonous.)*

With a grown-up's help, search through the kitchen cupboards and the refrigerator to see how many other things you eat that contain minerals.

Nutrition Facts	
Serving size: 1/2 cup (58g)	
Servings per container: 8	

Amount Per Serving	
Calories 200	
Calories from Fat 10	

	% Daily Value
Total Fat 1g	
Saturated Fat 0g	2%
Polyunsaturated Fat 0.5g	
Monounsaturated Fat 0g	
Cholesterol 0mg	0%
Sodium 350mg	15%
Potassium 160mg	5%
Total Carbohydrates 47g	16%
Dietary Fiber 5g	20%
Sugars 7g	
Other Carbohydrates 35g	
Protein 6g	

Vitamin A 15%	•	Vitamin C 0%
Calcium 2%	•	Iron 45%
Vitamin D 10%	•	Thiamin 25%
Riboflavin		25%
Niacin 25%	•	Vitamin B6 25%
Folate		25%
Vitamin B12		25%
Phosphorus		15%
Magnesium		15%
Zinc 8%	•	Copper 10%

Carbon, the Chameleon

Carbon, a very common natural material found on earth, appears as two different minerals with very different qualities — making it twice as useful!

One mineral, called *graphite,* is soft and black. You use soft, slippery graphite every day in school — it's the lead in most of our pencils! The mineral graphite is plentiful, so pencils are inexpensive.

But when carbon appears in another mineral form, we consider it very beautiful and valuable. It's hard to imagine that the clear, sparkly *diamond* is the same mineral as a pencil point, but it's true! Diamonds are used to make jewelry, of course, and because diamonds are the hardest natural substance we've found on earth, the blades of certain types of saws and even some fingernail files have diamond dust on them.

THAT WILL BE FIVE ROCKS, PLEASE!

Can you imagine having to lug a big rock to school to buy milk at lunchtime? The people on the Pacific island of Yap used to use huge pieces of limestone rock as big as 12 feet (3.5 m) across as their money! Fortunately for us, most countries use small metal coins for money.

The names for some coins in the United States have gotten kind of mixed up over the years, however. For example, a nickel is mostly made from copper. But the "copper" penny is really bronze, which is a mixture of mostly copper with a little zinc thrown in. And "silver" dollars no longer have any silver in them. Go figure!

Answer: A pearl forms when a grain of sand gets trapped inside an oyster's shell. The oyster produces a special type of spit that covers the sand, making it rounder and softer.

Start a Coin Collection!

Want to collect some hard metals and have some fun, too? Begin collecting coins! One way to start is to go to a bank where they have foreign currency (money) you can exchange for your country's currency. Sort your coins by country, by size and shape, or by metal types. Some have holes punched in them, or faces and animals inscribed, and dates stamped on them. They're like having a little piece of that country's history right in your pocket!

Think About It!

Placing Value

What makes gold worth more than silver? And platinum worth more than gold? In the world of value, two things matter: *supply* (how much there is) and *demand* (how much people want it). If everyone wants something (demand), and there isn't enough to go around (supply), people are willing to pay more to get it. Sometimes it doesn't make any sense, but that's the way it works.

1 dollar • Singapore

50 pence • United Kingdom

1 pound • United Kingdom

1 ringgit • Malaysia

1 quarter • Canada

50 sen • Malaysia

1 Susan B. Anthony dollar • U.S.

10 sen • Malaysia

Honesty Wins Again!

In the 1800s, Russia, Colombia, and the United States used gold and silver in their coins. While searching for gold, miners sometimes found a very heavy, silvery metal called *platinum*. People hadn't come up with a use for this new metal yet, so it was very inexpensive.

Some people figured out they could use platinum to make *counterfeit*, or fake, money. They covered a thick layer of platinum with a thin layer of expensive gold.

But guess what? The trick was on the counterfeiters, because nowadays platinum is a very valuable metal that is worth a lot more than gold! Having one of those counterfeit platinum coins today is better than having a real gold coin!

Shopping Cart Caper!

It's a Saturday morning, and you're at one of your favorite places — the grocery store! Mom stops to chat with a neighbor, so you take the list and the cart, ready to roll. Oh, and by the way, your mom is a geologist, so the list looks a little unusual! Can you find all the items?

Shopping List

1 gallon calcium

sodium chloride (small box)

2 packages of fluoride

clay pellets (large bag)

cardboard strip with diamond dust

dried lava (1 chunk)

box of phosphorus, magnesium, zinc, copper, iron, and calcium (honey-nut flavored)

For school supplies:

1 box graphite

1 box limestone (assorted colors, please)

For camping trip:

zinc oxide (1 tube)

box of phosphorus and sulfur

A Mineral Recipe ... for You!

Hold up a mirror and take a good look at yourself. Do you see curly or straight hair? Freckles? Now, put on those geologist's eyes for a closer look. Surprise! Your body contains as much

**calcium as 340 sticks of chalk,
phosphorus and sulfur as 2,500 boxes of matches,
sodium and chlorine as 40 teaspoons (200 ml) of salt,
fluoride as 30 tubes of toothpaste,
iron as 6 paper clips,
potassium as 500 bananas,
magnesium as 182 antacid tablets.**

You've got a little zinc, copper, cobalt, and iodine, and lots of carbon too!
  See what a rich geological treasure you are? You and the earth are both mineral masterpieces!

Answers: milk, salt, toothpaste, cat litter, fingernail file, pumice stone, Cheerios, pencils, chalk, sunblock, matches.

13

Earth-Treasures Scavenger Hunt

Now that you've taken a good look inside the earth's treasure chest, you're ready for a scavenger hunt. Your mission: to gather earth treasures from all over your house. Don't forget all the places you can search: the kitchen, the bathroom, the home office, the garage, and the basement or workshop. You might find some objects that are too big to move (just write those down on a piece of paper). Ready? Here are your clues!

◉ You need these earth metals to use a pay phone or go through a tollbooth.

◉ Spikes of these earth minerals help hold your house together.

◉ Your parents reach for a clear cylinder full of this earth mineral when you feel hot and flushed.

◉ You use this earth mineral to hold your book report together.

◉ You get a blast of vitamin C as well as this earth mineral when you drink a glass of this juice.

◉ Babies like a dusting of this earth mineral after their bath.

◉ You rip off a sheet of this earth metal to cover a casserole in the oven.

◉ A flashlight and cell phone operate with the help of this earth mineral.

Bonus clues:

◉ The inside walls of your house might be made of this earth mineral.

◉ These earth materials help you play your favorite computer games.

◉ This earth metal carries electricity into your house.

◉ A thin layer of this very shiny earth mineral might cover a part of your stove.

Answers: copper, zinc, bronze, silver, nickel (quarters, dimes, pennies, nickels); iron and iron (nails); mercury (thermometer); zinc and iron (paper clips or staples); calcium (calcium-fortified orange juice); talc (powder); aluminum (aluminum foil); nickel (rechargeable battery). Bonus: gypsum (Sheetrock); gold (computer contacts) and silicon (computer chips); copper (wire); chromium (oven-door handle)

THE FIRST ROCK GROUP

O K, yes, geology is also about rocks, as in huge cliffs, little pebbles, tiny grains of sand, and particles of soil. How did they end up all over the place?

To find out, let's take a tour of the biggest rock factory in the world. Did you know you're standing on it? We're talking about earth, of course! You'll compare the different ways melted minerals harden into rock. You'll see what happens when many layers of rock-forming earth materials press together over millions of years (don't worry, we can speed that up a little!). You'll follow a grain of sand on its journey to becoming a rock — hundreds of miles away from where it started (but you won't leave your house). And you'll meet the first rock group — Igneous "Iggy," Sedimentary "Sed," and Metamorphic "Morph"! So, ready to rock?

A BIRD'S-EYE VIEW

Good morning, folks, and welcome to Sightseeing Sam's Tours of the West! On your right, we have the Cascades, a mountain range that stretches from northern California across Oregon and Washington up into Canada, and that beautiful snow-capped peak in southern Washington is Mount Saint Helens.

But what's this? It looks as if the north side of the mountain is starting to crumble! Yes, the top of the mountain just blew off! Wow!

Was that a rock the size of a car that just shot out of the top? It must have been traveling about 200 miles per hour (320 kph)! Hold on tight — we're going closer for a better look! Now there's a gray cloud billowing *way* up into the sky, while rock and ash are pouring down the sides of the mountain. Uh-oh! Here comes the mud, covering everything in sight! It looks just like concrete! Whew! What a sight!

Blowing and Flowing!

When Mount Saint Helens exploded in 1980, it was the most destructive volcano in the history of the United States! When the ash and mud stopped flowing, the sides of the mountain and much of the surrounding area looked like the moon, covered with a thick gray layer. But when everything cooled down, what was lying around all over the place? Brand-new rocks!

Car about 10 miles from eruption

Mailboxes near the Cowlitz River, Washington

Mount Saint Helens • May 18, 1980, eruption

Mount Saint Helens • April 27, 1990

WHAT'S COOKIN'?

When a grown-up opens the oven door to check on your batch of chocolate chip cookies, you have to stand back from the blast of heat. A 325°F (160°C) oven is hot! Well, imagine a blast of heat 10 times hotter, and you'll get an idea of how hot it is deep inside the earth — so hot that the minerals have melted, much the way the chips in your cookies do.

Those melted minerals inside the earth form a red-hot liquid called *magma* (see page 47). It's churning around with lots of steam and gases, under incredible pressure from the weight of all the layers on top. When the magma finds a weak spot in the earth's outer layer, it pushes its way through and comes bursting out, just like a big burp! We call magma that flows onto the earth's surface *lava.* That's what went on inside Mount Saint Helens to cause such a powerful explosion.

Some lavas are:
- *light and foamy because they are full of gases and steam, shooting high in the air*
- *thick and smooth, oozing slowly over the ground*
- *very runny, flowing quickly and quietly along*
- *lumpy with chunks of minerals and rock*
- *gritty with lots of volcanic ash in them*

Lava Lingo!

"Darn, I've got slurry all over my boots!"
"Watch out for that cow-dung bomb!"
If you were a geologist, you'd get to talk like this all the time when you were describing lava!

Bleb: a small bit of material in the lava (think of a blob).
Slurry: a muddy lava.
Spatter: splashes when it lands.
Cow-dung bomb: Well, ever walked through a cow pasture? Imagine if one of those "piles" that are all over the place had dropped out of the sky and landed at your feet!

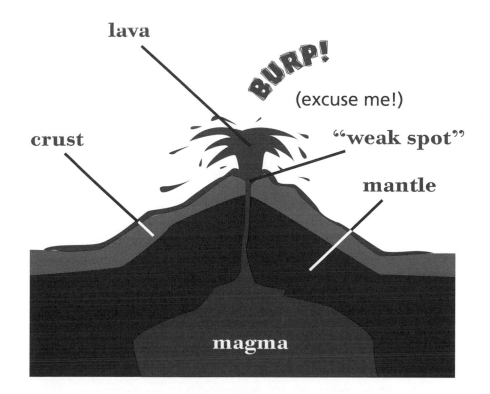

lava

BURP!

(excuse me!)

crust

"weak spot"

mantle

magma

MEET IGGY!

Iggy will help you remember about *igneous rocks*, the rocks that form when melted minerals cool down and harden. But not all igneous rocks are created with a dramatic display like Mount Saint Helens. Sometimes magma flows through cracks away from all the volcanic activity to another place underground where it cools down slowly inside the earth. Magma can also bubble up through a crack in the ocean floor and then cool down and solidify into rock under the sea (page 50).

Do you think igneous rocks formed in these different ways will have the same appearance? Let's see!

You gotta go with the flow...

Sugar on a Sheet

Grease a baking sheet and put it in the freezer to chill. Put ¹/₂ cup (125 ml) of sugar in a saucepan. With a grown-up's help, stir the sugar over medium heat. When it is completely melted, take the baking sheet out of the freezer and pour the melted sugar on it. Put the sheet back in the freezer. After a few minutes, take the sheet out and look at your sugar glass.

Sugar on a Stick

Mix 1 cup (250 ml) sugar and ½ cup (125 ml) water in a saucepan. With a grown-up's help, stir the mixture over low heat until the sugar dissolves. When it starts to boil, stop stirring and let the mixture boil for 1 minute. Set a Popsicle stick in a glass. Ask your grown-up helper to pour the syrup into the glass and place it where it can cool slowly. Check on it every few days.

After a few days, examine your sugar stick. How does it compare with your sugar glass? How could you explain the different formations? Hint: Think about how the two sugar rocks cooled.

It's Crystal Clear Now!

What makes igneous rocks look so different from one another? When lava cools quickly on the earth's surface or magma cools on the ocean floor, as the syrup did in the freezer, the crystals in the minerals (see page 36) form very quickly, so they're small (sometimes you can't even see them). But when the magma cools slowly deep inside the earth, as on the Popsicle stick, large crystals have time to form, and you can see them in the rock when you examine it. Cool, huh?

Is There a Volcano in Your Neighborhood?

Well, maybe not a live one, but it's likely there are lots of volcanic rocks around you, anyway.

◉ Take a walk with a grown-up friend around town (bring along a magnifying glass, paper, and a crayon). See if you can spot any large public buildings or monuments made from the igneous rock *granite*. Can you see crystals (with or without the magnifying glass)? If it's unpolished rock, place the paper over the surface, and rub with the crayon. Do you see any patterns in the rubbing you made? If you see ripples (like those in cake batter) or holes, they could be from the flowing magma that formed the rock!

"Giant" Granite
Relative of Iggy
Appearance: large particles easily seen; speckled light and dark
Color: white to gray, pink, red
Where it occurs naturally: mountains throughout North America

Granite • Library of Congress • Washington, D.C.

◉ As you ride in the car or hike in the woods, watch for clues that Iggy is here — huge, exposed slabs of rough, gray rock or boulder piles that look as if they'd be fun to climb on. Such outcroppings are often granite — a sign that magma was around long ago!

◉ The ornamental stone used to decorate fancy buildings might be the volcanic rock *basalt*. Throughout the western United States near active or former volcanoes, you can see cliffs of basalt.

Language Links

Don't Blow Your Top!

Long ago, people thought that volcanoes were alive, and their eruptions were a sign that they were angry. So people started using the same image when a person lost his or her temper, saying he was "blowing his top." When people lose their tempers, they often do or say things that hurt others. When you get really angry, what are some other ways to "let off steam" without blowing your top?

Rock Stars!

Devils Tower, Wyoming
What if the magma comes up to the earth's surface — but it just can't push through? Devils Tower is all that's left of an ancient volcano. The magma hardened and the soil covering it wore away, leaving a solid tower of igneous rock.

"Bubbles" Basalt
Relative of Iggy
Appearance: fine grained, may have some large crystals; can have "bubbly" surface
Color: dark gray to black, dark brown to reddish brown
Where it occurs naturally: where volcanoes are or have been active; widespread in large portions of western United States

Where might you find more volcano products right in your own home? Hint: Think about where really sturdy, rock-hard materials were used to build your house. If you're heading for the basement, you're on the right track! Concrete (page 88) feels rough and gritty because it is made with cement, which can contain volcanic ash. Iggy's here again!

Rocks on the Move!

Take a pinch of sand or soil and spread it out on a piece of white paper. Look at it closely (use a magnifying glass, if you like). What are those little round pieces? Tiny rocks! In fact, you might be looking at pieces of an igneous rock from a volcanic blast thousands of years ago (especially if you live in the western United States). What happened to make it so small? And how did it get all the way to your neighborhood?

Well, you might think rocks have a pretty boring life, sitting around waiting for someone to send them skipping across a pond or worse, to kick them. Not true! Rocks get around! They are constantly moving and changing, even without our help.

Whee!!

CLACK!

CLACK!

CLICK!

It's a Hard (Rock's) Life!

After a volcano erupts, that igneous rock might hang out on the side of the mountain for a while (we're talking several hundred years here). Maybe a bear walks by and knocks it loose, and as it bounces and bumps down the mountain, a tiny piece breaks off. The pebble hangs out for another few hundred years, baking in the summer sun and freezing in the winter rain. Little cracks start to develop. One day you come along. You grab the little rock and toss it into a stream. It settles to the bottom, where the flowing water bumps it against a nearby rock for a long time.

Try it! Write the next chapter in this rock's history, following it on its journey to becoming a tiny grain of sand. Think about thousands of years of summer droughts and winter storms — maybe even an earthquake or two! And don't forget the actions of animals and people, too!

A RECYCLING BIN FOR ROCKS?

Did you think people invented recycling? Nature is way ahead of us on that one! When old rocks, shells, bones, plant parts, and other bits of material (called *sediment*) are pressed together until they harden, they are "recycled" into new rocks called *sedimentary rocks*. These particles can be moved a long way by water or air first, but eventually they settle out and land somewhere. As more and more sediment piles up, over thousands and thousands of years, the weight of the top layers presses the lower layers into rock.

Lay it on me, man...

Scouting for Sed

Sed, our hard-pressed sedimentary rock friend, is often found where sediment settles.

Has Sed settled near you? See how many different types of sediment you can find! Hint: Sediment can land indoors or out, and the pieces can be big or small.

The Weather (ing) Forecast

When the sun, wind, water, plants, or animals wear away rocks and minerals, breaking them into smaller pieces, it's called **weathering**. *When these tiny pieces are moved from one place to another by wind or water, it's called* **erosion**.

How Do *You* Say Sediment?

Many types of sediment have special names, but they are still sediments. What are these sediments called?

- **Sediment that falls out of the air onto furniture or the floor**

- **Sediment that falls out of the air when it is cold outside**

- **Sediment in some types of orange juice**

- **Sediment in the bottom of a wine bottle**

- **Sediment left behind in the coffee pot**

Here's a tougher one!
- **Sediment deposited near the edge of a glacier (it might include boulders bigger than you!)**

Answers: dust, snow, pulp, dregs, grinds, glacial till

Settle Down!

Many sedimentary rocks look a little bit like an earth sandwich — a layer of this, a layer of that.

Fill a clear jar with pebbles, sand, twigs, and leaves. Add 1/4 cup (50 ml) Epsom salts (available at a drugstore). Add water until there is only about 2 inches (5 cm) of space left at the top. Put the jar lid on tight and shake. Once all the ingredients — oops, make that sediments, because they are now floating in water — are thoroughly mixed, place the jar on a flat surface.

Check on your jar every hour or so. Can you guess which sediments will drop to the bottom first? Can you see layers forming? This layered look is caused by different types of sediment settling down at different times. Was your guess about what would be on the bottom correct?

Carefully pour the water out of the jar and let the layers dry completely. Congratulations! You are the proud owner of a homemade sedimentary rock!

Sticking Together

The sedimentary rock recipe above includes dissolved minerals that stick the sediment together. Epsom salts (the minerals magnesium and sulfur) is the glue that holds your homemade rock together!

Be a Sand Sculptor!

Sand compressed for millions of years becomes sandstone. *All around the world, this sedimentary rock is sculpted into amazing formations by the eroding forces of wind and water blasting away at it. Act like a force of nature and create your own sandstone sculpture!*

You will need:
- 🪨 **2 cups (500 ml) of sand**
- 🪨 **1 cup (250 ml) of water**
- 🪨 **1 cup (250 ml) of cornstarch**
- 🪨 **An old saucepan**
- 🪨 **Paint (optional)**

1. *Combine the sand, water, and cornstarch in the pan. With a grown-up's help, heat the mixture slowly until it's thick.*
2. *Let it cool; then, use your hands to mold it. Let your sculpture dry and harden. Then, paint it to create your own Bryce Canyon!*

What a Waste!

Rock Stars!

Bryce Canyon National Park, Utah
"Red rocks standing like men" is how the Paiute Indians described these sedimentary rock formations of red, pink, and white sandstone and limestone, shaped by wind and water.

A Sedimentary Stroll

A Pyggy Bank?

Why do some people save their money in a piggy bank? It all started in the 1400s when people made their dishes and jars out of a type of clay called *pygg*. Sometimes families would have a special "pygg jar" to save their money in. After many years, people forgot that "pygg" meant a type of clay. So when someone would ask a potter to make them a "pyggy" bank, he or she would make it in the shape of a pig!

"Sandy" Sandstone
Relative of Sed
Appearance: **fine to medium particles; rough, gritty feel**
Color: **gray; red, brown**
Where it occurs naturally: **western United States**

- If you're in or near a city in the eastern United States, ask a grown-up to take you for a walk in a residential neighborhood of houses called "brownstones" (a type of *sandstone*). What color are these buildings? How would you describe the surfaces?

- Sometimes large public buildings are made of *limestone,* a grayish rock with a rough, gritty surface. If you find any in your town, look closely for fossils!

- When you walk on a sidewalk, you're walking on crushed *limestone,* one of the materials mixed with cement to make concrete. Cliffs and caves are examples of natural limestone formations.

- Here's something to watch for on the highway: places where rock ledges have been blasted away. You may see different-colored layers of *sedimentary rock*.

- Clay is a sediment often found along the shores of lakes and rivers. See if you can spot clay in two different forms: as *shale,* a clay-based sedimentary rock, and as manmade clay bricks.
  Try it! *Look for natural clay deposits and squeeze the murky mud into shapes — it molds just like storebought clay!*

Limestone · Notre Dame cathedral · Paris, France

YOU'VE HEARD OF GHOST WRITING ...

What about "skeleton" writing? Does the thought of holding animal bones give you the creeps? Well, when you draw or write with chalk, you're doing just that!

Pure chalk is *limestone*, a sedimentary rock made from the shell-like skeletons of tiny sea animals. Graveyards of millions of these animals, like the famous White Cliffs of Dover on the coast of England, are just great big piles of chalk.

But to be honest, even though we still call it chalk, what you write with at school isn't made from limestone anymore. It's usually made from the mineral *gypsum*, another sedimentary rock that makes a mark just like chalk but is less expensive.

"Smooth-talkin'" Shale
Relative of Sed
Appearance: smooth and fine grained; particles are not visible; may contain fossils!
Color: usually gray, also brown, reddish brown, deep red, or black
Where it occurs naturally: widespread throughout North America; often occurs near sandstone

"Bones" Limestone
Relative of Sed
Appearance: fine grained, with a pitted, crumbly-looking surface that may contain fossils!
Color: light gray to dark gray, sometimes with some yellow and brown
Where it occurs naturally: mountainous areas of North America; coastal cliffs; reefs; caves

WHAT'S NEXT?

Your rock started off being blasted out of a volcano and ended up as a grain of sand that turned into a sedimentary rock. What on earth is going to happen to this rock next? Well, it could just stay a sedimentary rock. Or, if conditions were right, it could get hotter and hotter and feel more and more pressure until it "morphs," or changes, right into another kind of rock — a *metamorphic rock!*

You may already know the word *metamorphosis* — it's used to describe the change a caterpillar goes through to become a butterfly. *Meta*, which comes from the Greek word for "after," means "change." *Morphe* means "form," like the Mighty Morphin Power Rangers, cartoon superheroes who can change their form.

Whoa, I'm HOT! I can't take all this PRESSURE! How much more TIME do I have to spend here?

MEET MORPH!

When igneous or sedimentary rocks buried deep in the earth are squeezed together for millions of years, what happens to them? Just ask Morph!

Try it! Fill a bowl with fresh snow or crushed ice. Using your bare hands, press the snow or ice into a ball. Keep pressing for a full minute until the ball is small. Take another look at the ball. Is it harder or softer? What would happen to it if you only melted it on top of a stove (heat)? What would happen to it if you hit it with a hammer (pressure)? What would happen if you used heat and pressure, but only for 5 or 10 seconds?

If rocks only get hot, they melt and are magma again, so any new rocks they make are igneous rocks. If rocks are put under pressure without enough heat or time, they just break apart, and nothing really changes except their size. To make a metamorphic rock, you need all three conditions: heat + pressure + time.

It Looks Marble-ous!

Unwrap two different-colored pieces of soft candy like taffy or Starbursts, and put one on top of the other. Wrap them up in waxed paper and squeeze them as tightly as you can for several minutes. Open your hands and look at the pieces carefully. If you were squeezing together two pieces of limestone, they'd be metamorphosing into marble, *a common metamorphic rock with swirls of color throughout!*

Marblelize Before Your Eyes!

Marbled paper is different colors all swirled around on one sheet. Make your own and see!

"Marvelous" Marble
Relative of Morph
Appearance: grainy surface with "folds" and "bends" that occur during metamorphosis
Color: pure marble is white; other minerals add characteristic swirls of color
Where it occurs naturally: mountains of North America

Fill a shallow baking pan half full of water. Cover the pan with a screen. Rub colored chalk across the screen (three colors work best). Swirl the chalk lightly with your finger.

Now, dip a large piece of construction paper into the water to "pick up" the chalk. Lay your marbleized paper flat, chalk side up, to dry.

Rockin' Along the Boulevard

To search for relatives of Morph, start by looking for the fanciest buildings around town, like banks, big hotels, or museums. Check out floors and big columns of these buildings, too.

- Keep an eye out for stone statues in parks or in front of public buildings. Do they have the swirly pattern of marble, or the sparkly look of granite?

- Take a walk through a cemetery (with a grown-up friend). See if you can pick out tombstones made from marble or *slate,* a metamorphic rock made from shale. Now see if you can find a limestone (sedimentary) tombstone with the same year on it. How has the lettering held up on the sedimentary rock compared with the metamorphic rocks?

Marble • The Lincoln Memorial • Washington, D.C.

- See any stone roofs (especially in older neighborhoods) or walkways made from flat, smooth rocks? Years ago, slate was commonly used as a roofing material. When slate is used for a patio or path, it's called *flagstone.*

    Try it! *Write or draw a picture on some flagstone with chalk (ask permission first). What do you think slate was used for in the classroom of 100 years ago?*

"Slick" Slate
Relative of Morph
Appearance: fine grained; sparkly mica sometimes visible with magnifying glass
Color: gray, black, green, brown, red, or purple
Where it occurs naturally: mountains of North America

Rock Stars!

Marble quarries, Carrara, Italy
Huge deposits of marble formed when the Apennines mountains in central Italy were created. Carrara marble is prized all over the world for its beautiful colors and swirling patterns.

Rockology!

Now you know the ways that rocks are made. But that's just the beginning of the secrets they hold. Ready to become a real rock expert?

The next time you're in the backyard or walking to school, stop and pick up a rock. Really take a look at it. Turn it over and over in your hands. Feel the surface — is it rough? Smooth? A little of both? What colors does it have in it? Is it sparkly? Can you pick or scratch off any pieces? Try making a mark with your rock on another rock — what does the mark look like?

Geologists always have their eyes open for cool-looking rocks. And when they find one, they do all the things you just did, and it tells them a lot about that particular rock. They do a few more simple tests, too, most of which you can do right at home. So let's go rock hunting!

Calling All Rock Hounds!

A hound is a type of dog used for hunting because it has a very sharp sense of smell and can really follow a scent. Rock hounds are people who are hot on the trail of awesome rocks, always adding to their collections!

Starting a collection of special stones is easy, because rocks are just about everywhere. You don't need much in the way of equipment, either — good observation skills, several small plastic bags, and a pencil and paper so you can keep notes about where you found each sample. Look for rocks of different sizes and shapes, and those with interesting colors and markings. Collect rocks from a variety of places and "backgrounds" (diversity makes things more interesting in the rock world, too!).

Keep an eye out for the perfect lucky stone to carry in your pocket, and choose a few hefty paperweights to keep your desktop tidy. And you can't have too many small, flat specimens for skipping across the water.

Rock Belly Flops!

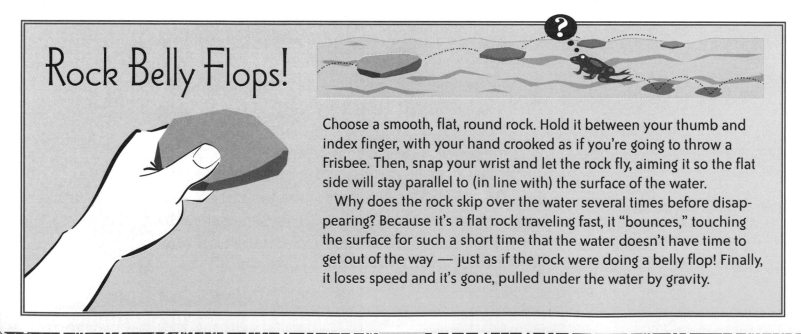

Choose a smooth, flat, round rock. Hold it between your thumb and index finger, with your hand crooked as if you're going to throw a Frisbee. Then, snap your wrist and let the rock fly, aiming it so the flat side will stay parallel to (in line with) the surface of the water.

Why does the rock skip over the water several times before disappearing? Because it's a flat rock traveling fast, it "bounces," touching the surface for such a short time that the water doesn't have time to get out of the way — just as if the rock were doing a belly flop! Finally, it loses speed and it's gone, pulled under the water by gravity.

Sort It Out!

Think about your friends or classmates. How would you describe them? How would you describe yourself? Maybe your self-description reads something like this: girl, red-haired, broken arm, 4 1/2 feet (1.4 m) tall, and 10 years old. Put all that information together, and it describes a unique person — you!

But what do you notice when you compare your self-description with your descriptions of your friends? What are some of the descriptive words that you all share? What are some of the different ways to sort your friends into groups? Would you sort yourself into the curly-haired group or the brown-eyed 10-year-old group, or both groups?

continued >

Tricks of the Trade

Have you ever tried to pick up a large rock or even to roll one across the yard? Rocks are heavy! But in movies, you see superheroes pick up huge boulders and throw them a long way. Sometimes, moviemakers cut and paint large pieces of Styrofoam-like material to make them look like rocks. The real trick is for the actors to make it look as if the rocks are very heavy — even though they hardly weigh anything at all!

Now look through your rock samples to see how many different ways you can sort them. Try grouping them first by color, by size, by how rough or smooth they are, or by the streaks or markings on the outside. Does each rock belong in only one group? Rocks aren't so different from people, you see!

When geologists sort rocks in the lab, however, they don't use characteristics like size or shape — these vary too much to be an accurate way to identify a rock. Instead, geologists group rocks that are made of the same earth ingredients together and give that group a name, like granite or limestone.

Think About It!

You Can't Judge a Book by Its Cover

Have you ever heard that expression? It means that appearances don't tell the whole story. It's what is inside that counts — inside your mind, head, and personality, inside a book, and inside a rock, too!

THE BUILDING BLOCKS OF ROCKS

Remember those minerals that you gathered from all over your house (see page 14)? Minerals are not only those useful earth materials we use over and over every day, *they are also the ingredients that make up all rocks.* Some rocks, like limestone, have just one mineral (in this case, *calcite*). Another common rock, granite, is made up mostly of the minerals *quartz* and *feldspar*, with a few others, like *mica*, mixed in. Most of the rocks on earth are made from about 20 minerals — pretty amazing when you consider there are more than 2,500 minerals that we've discovered so far!

Minerals are easy to identify. That's why geologists begin their rock identification tests by figuring out the minerals that are in a rock sample. So let's be geologists and crack open the clues inside those rocks!

I'm a lot of quartz, I'm a lot of feldspar, I'm a little bit mica, I'm a little bit ...

Is that hard rock?

granite

Break It Up!

Wrap one of your rock samples in an old towel or pillowcase. (Note: Very important! Wear a pair of safety glasses or a snorkeling mask.) Place the wrapped rock on a hard surface, such as your driveway or a sidewalk, and strike it as hard as you can with a hammer. Now, open the towel.

Did the rock crumble into tiny sandlike pieces, split in half, or shatter into sharp pieces? Maybe you couldn't break it apart, no matter how hard you hit it. Try several other different-looking rocks and compare the results.

How hard or easy it is to smash a rock depends on what minerals it contains. When a mineral breaks into smooth, flat pieces, geologists say it *cleaves.* If it breaks into rough or jagged pieces, they say it *fractures.*

Different samples of the same mineral will always break apart the same way. Geologists can usually tell what mineral they're looking at just by breaking it apart and observing whether or not it cleaves. (They will say it *has cleavage*, or it *lacks cleavage.)*

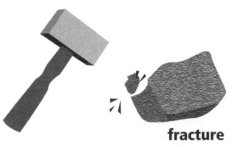

fracture

cleavage

The Strong and the Weak

Whether you smash a tiny fragment of quartz or a huge chunk, both will break apart in a way that's particular to quartz. But smash up two pieces of mica, and they will break apart in a way that's particular to mica (and different from quartz). What determines how these minerals break apart? The materials that make up each mineral form in a particular pattern called a *crystal*. Big piece of mineral or small — the materials inside that mineral always repeat in the same formation to create these crystals.

Some crystals are very strong — the individual pieces hug each other tightly because they have strong *bonds* (the "connectors" holding the pieces together). Other crystals are weak with flimsy connectors — it doesn't take much to knock them apart. So, it's not surprising that a rock made of minerals with weak crystals shatters into bits when you hit it with a hammer, while one with tight, strong connectors is harder to break apart.

Sort your samples into those that have minerals with strong crystals or weak ones.

Pebble Play

Abbé René Just Haüy

Can you imagine making a revolutionary discovery about minerals simply by dropping one on the floor and observing the way it broke? That's exactly what Abbé René Just Haüy (aw-WEE), a French priest who also studied minerals, did!

In 1781, he dropped a piece of calcite on the floor and noticed that each fragment broke with the same number of smooth sides and angles. From that simple observation, Haüy proposed that minerals have a repeating pattern inside that makes each type always break apart the same way. His discovery proves once again that sharp eyes and a thoughtful mind are the most important tools for unearthing science secrets!

The game mancala has been played all over the world for thousands of years! In Africa, kids use pebbles and a "gameboard" of shallow holes scooped out of the ground. You can play the traditional way, or make your own gameboard.

Try it! Cut the lid of an egg carton in half, and tape or staple one section to each end. Place 4 pebbles in each of the 12 egg cups, leaving the two "mancala bins" on the ends empty. Set the board between two players. Flip a coin (or a stone) to decide who goes first. Your goal is to move the most stones into your mancala.

To take a turn, pick up all the stones in any one of your small bins, and drop them, one by one in a counterclockwise direction, into each bin around the board. If you pass your mancala, drop a stone in, but don't drop one into the other player's mancala. If the last stone falls in your mancala, take another turn.

If the last stone falls in an empty bin on your side, put all the stones from the bin directly across from that bin, plus the capturing stone, into your mancala. If you touch your stones (to count them, for example), then you must play them.

The game ends when one player runs out of stones in his small bins. The other player gets to place any remaining stones in her bins into her mancala. The player with the most stones wins.

Can Your Rocks Pass the Scratch Test?

Usually we have to be careful not to scratch things. But when you're being a geologist, you get to make scratches with your rocks on purpose! You begin with a soft object and try harder and harder ones. Whether or not you can make a mark is another way of learning about the minerals in your rocks.

Take one piece of each of your sample rocks and see if you can scratch their surfaces with your fingernail. Then try the penny. (You can scratch the rock with the penny or the penny with the rock, whichever is easier.) Next, try scratching it with the table knife. Do any of your rocks make a scratch on the glass? Ask a grown-up if you could try it with a steel file (a workshop tool).

Geologists use the scratch test *to see how hard a mineral is by scratching that mineral with other minerals. The 10 minerals geologists use for the scratch test are numbered from softest (1) to hardest (10) on a scale called* Mohs' *scale of hardness. Most minerals on earth fall between 3 and 7 on Mohs' scale. See where your rocks fall!*

You will need:
- Penny
- Dull table knife
- Old drinking glass
- Steel file (optional)

I should have used harder stone.

Hard Choices

Why is it helpful to know how hard a mineral is? Could you use a rock that is only a 2 or 3 on Mohs' scale to make a gravel driveway? When would you want to use a mineral that was soft? How about choosing stone for a stone house?

Powder Soft or Diamond Hard?

Mohs' Scale of Hardness

1=softest
10=hardest

Talc	1	leaves greasy flakes on fingers
Gypsum	2	scratched by fingernail
Calcite	3	scratched by penny
Fluorite	4	scratched easily by knife
Apatite	5	not scratched easily by knife
Orthoclase	6	scratched by file
Quartz	7	scratches glass easily
Topaz	8	scratches glass easily
Corundum	9	scratches glass easily
Diamond	10	scratches all other materials

Great Geologists!

Friedrich Mohs

In 1812, Friedrich Mohs, an Austrian scientist who worked with minerals, suggested that all geologists use the same 10 minerals for the scratch test so that scientists would be able to compare the results accurately from any lab in the world. Mohs started with the softest mineral, talc (like baby powder, which is mostly talc) and called that 1. Then he chose nine other minerals of increasing hardness, right on up to 10, the diamond, which is the hardest mineral on earth. It can only be scratched by another diamond!

Mineral Matchup!

OK, sports fans. In one corner you've got "Crusher" Quartz; in the other, Mica the "Flake." When they butt heads, who will be left standing? Here are their stats:

"Crusher" Quartz
smash test: **difficult to break apart; prone to fractures**
hardness scale : **7**

Mica the "Flake"
smash test: **has cleavage**
hardness scale: **2 to 2.5**

Answer: If you're rooting for quartz, you're a winner!

Streakers!

Cleavage, hardness, and now streaks! These geologists sure do speak a strange language!

On the back (unglazed) side of a piece of white tile, press down with one of your rocks, and make a mark. What color is it? Is the mark (called a streak*) the same color as your rock? Try different rocks, then compare the colors.*

When geologists perform this test in the lab, they use a powdered sample of a mineral because it's much easier to identify the mineral from the color it leaves. They match the color of the streak to a mark in a reference book (see page 42). Pure quartz (colorless) and *amethyst* (a purple form of quartz) both leave a white streak. Shiny *pyrite* (also called fool's gold) leaves a greenish-black streak.

Play Rock Tic-Tac-Toe!

Congratulations! You've performed most of the major tests geologists do to identify the minerals that make up rocks. With what you've learned about rocks and minerals, can you tell how the rocks you collected were made?

On a piece of posterboard, make the gameboard shown here. See if you can fill in the board with your rocks.

Rock Tic-Tac-Toe

IGNEOUS	SEDIMENTARY	METAMORPHIC
Has many small holes	Has layers (and maybe even a fossil!)	Has swirled patterns
Very hard to smash	Breaks apart easily	Hard to smash
Has light and dark speckles and/or large visible crystals	Fizzes when you put a few drops of lemon juice or vinegar on it*	Has an all-over shininess (rather than speckles)

* These weak acids dissolve calcium carbonate, a major ingredient in many sedimentary rocks.

THE NAME GAME

When geologists name a new rock, they usually make up a name based on the minerals in the rock. (*Zincite* is named for its main ingredient — zinc.) But when the astronauts of Apollo 11 (July 1969) returned from the moon with rock samples, they discovered several of them had combinations of minerals different from any rock that had been discovered on earth so far. The rock was named *armalcolite* after the three astronauts — Neil *Arm*strong, Buzz *Al*drin, and Michael *Col*lins — who had been on the flight. Very clever!

Try it! Choose several of your favorite or your most awesome-looking rocks and give them names. Maybe you'll name one after yourself (with a name like Katycite or Markolite) or after the friends who were with you when you

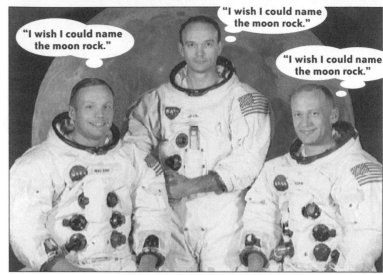

Apollo 11 astronauts (left to right): Armstrong, Collins, Aldrin

found the rock. Or maybe you were vacationing in a special place when it caught your eye, so give it a name that will bring back memories of where you were when you found the rock (like Oregonite).

ARM+AL+COL+ITE

Digging Deeper

Research your rocks in a guide to rocks and minerals! Here are two from the National Audubon Society that have lots of information as well as great photos to help you identify your finds: *Familiar Rocks & Minerals of North America* (a NAS Pocket Guide) or *Rocks and Minerals* (a NAS First Field Guide).

Or check them out online!

● **Rockhounds Information Page:**
  www.rahul.net/infodyn/rockhounds/rockhounds.html
● **Rockhounding in National Forests:**
  www.fs.fed.us/oonf/minerals/welcome.htm

For a mineral streak reference, check out *Rocks & Minerals* (Golden Books).

Catch a Falling Star!

You've collected some pretty cool rocks here on earth. But did you know you can collect some rocks from outer space, too? Tiny meteorites (particles of rock that fall from space) are always dusting the earth, so there are probably some near your home! These micro-meteorites are usually smaller than the head of a pin, but fortunately, they have iron and nickel in them, so they are attracted to a magnet.

Try it! *Make your very own micro-meteorite collector!*

2. *Put a strong magnet inside the cup. Using the strings to hold the cup, walk along the cracks in sidewalks or along the edge of a paved road, keeping the cup just barely above the ground as shown. If you listen carefully, you might hear a tiny "clink" when magnetic objects stick to the bottom of your cup.*

1. *Punch three holes around the top rim of a paper cup. Poke a piece of string through each hole and tie a knot. Pull all three strings together above the cup and tie together.*

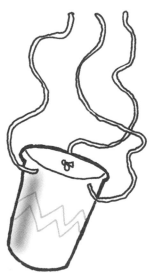

continued >

Gardening in Stone

In Japan and China, many people use rocks as an important element in the design of their gardens. They arrange stones to look like a river, or they stack some large rocks together to make a mini mountain. If they have found a special stone, they might put in it a big yard of colored sand, and then rake the sand into special patterns. People relax by looking at the rocks and remembering their connections to the natural world.

Try it! *You can make a mini stone garden with special rocks you collect. Fill a shallow bowl with sand. (Color the sand with a few drops of food coloring first if you like). Arrange one or two interesting-looking rocks on top of the sand. Use a comb to make patterns around the rock.*

3. *Hold your cup over a piece of white paper and lift the magnet out of the cup. The collected pieces will fall off the bottom onto the paper. Not everything you collect will be stardust. Some debris may be scraps from cars or bikes. But the round, dark, shiny pieces just might be micro-meteorites!*

The Sky Is Falling!

If meteorites are falling to earth all the time, why don't we get bonked on the head when we're walking around? Well, most of them burn up as they enter the earth's atmosphere, so we're just sprinkled with their dust as it drifts down. But large meteorites would certainly do some damage, like the one that landed in Arizona about 50,000 years ago. Meteor Crater is so huge that 20 football games could be played at the same time inside it, while 2 million fans watch from the rim!

Try it! *Fill a pie pan with flour. Place some small toy houses and cars in the flour to represent towns and highways. Now, sprinkle your town with "salt" micro-meteorites. Do they cause any damage? Next, drop a marble on the earth. How far does the flour fly? Is anything destroyed? Finally, drop a golf ball on top. Uh-oh, another Meteor Crater in the neighborhood!*

Keep on Rockin'!

Now you're a real "rockologist," with a collection you can add to whenever an interesting rock comes along! Keep your eyes peeled for more cool rocks, whether you're on vacation in another part of the country or just going for a walk around the block. And now that you can "see" what a real geologist sees, you'll be looking at your rocks in a whole new way!

QUAKIN', SHAKIN', AND SHAPIN'

Now you know how the surface of the earth ended up covered with sand and soil, as well as pebbles and boulders! But wait a minute! How about all those other formations, like mountains, valleys, islands, and oceans? What's going on under our feet to create the incredibly varied contours of the earth's surface? Can geology explain that, too? You bet!

FEEL THE EARTH MOVE UNDER YOUR FEET?

Although no one has ever been able to drill a hole to the middle of the earth (much less all the way to the other side), geologists have made some educated guesses about what is deep inside. For starters, you know that once you get below the layer of soil we walk on, things really start heating up — and moving around (page 17). But we aren't usually aware of these movements, unless the earth rumbles with the force of an earthquake or explodes with the power of a volcano! That's when mountains are born or the oceans are reshaped, dramatically changing the face of the earth again.

A Mini Earth Model

Cut a little slit in the marsh- mallow and stick the candy in the center. Place the marshmal- low on the toothpick. With a grown-up's help, melt the chips in the saucepan over very low heat, stirring them so they don't burn. Dip the marshmal- low in the melted chocolate, completely covering it. Set it on waxed paper to cool.

You've just made a mini earth! And to take a quick trip to the center of your earth, you'll just have to bite in — in the name of science, of course!

You will need:
- **Large marshmallow**
- **A peppermint candy**
- **Toothpick**
- **Saucepan**
- **¼ cup (50 g) of chocolate chips**
- **Waxed paper**

CHOCOLATE COATING
(CRUST)

MARSHMALLOW
(MANTLE)

PEPPERMINT CANDY
(CORE)

Layer by Layer

The outer layer (chocolate) is the earth's **crust** of rock, cov- ered, in most places, with soil. Just as with the real earth, it was formed from hot, melted material that cooled down and hardened. This thin crust is home for all life that we know.

The soft, gooey middle layer (marshmallow) is the earth's **mantle**. It's about 1,800 miles (3,000 km) thick, or about the distance you'd go if you drove halfway across the United States. It's made of magma (page 17).

When you strike the candy in the middle, you've hit the cen- ter of the earth, called the **core**. Scientists believe that the earth's core is a solid kernel of metal surrounded by a layer of liquid metal. The core is just a little bit thicker than the mantle and about 9,000°F (5,000°C) — almost as hot as the surface of the sun!

Pangaea Puzzle

On a map of the world, trace the continents. Cut out the shapes. Now, spread out the pieces in front of you. What do you notice about them? (Hint: Pretend you're working on a jigsaw puzzle.)

When geologists began looking at all the continents together, they noticed that they do, indeed, fit together like a giant puzzle. The rock types and formations along the continents' edges match up perfectly! So geologists concluded that about 240 million years ago, the seven continents were one giant continent. They've named it Pangaea (pan-JEE-ah), which comes from a Greek word meaning "all lands."

Great Geologists!

Alfred Wegener and Arthur Holmes

Imagine proposing a totally new idea that changed what we understood about the earth so much that all the textbooks had to be rewritten? In 1912, Alfred Wegener, a German geologist and arctic explorer, suggested the astounding idea that all the continents had been joined together at one time. He drew maps showing how huge scratches and gouges in rocky surfaces of Africa and South America, left by a glacier, matched up perfectly.

But many scientists at that time didn't accept Wegener's idea, because he couldn't explain what had caused the continents to drift apart.

Enter geologist Arthur Holmes. He proposed that the earth's mantle was a hot, soupy layer that the continents slide around on, which was confirmed by studying how the ocean floor is always reforming. Wegener's theory of continental drift profoundly altered our model of earth!

SLIP-SLIDING AWAY

How did the continents break apart? The earth's crust (page 47), rather than being one solid layer of rock, is actually made up of huge sections called *plates*. There are six major plates and seven smaller ones. These plates are always moving around, riding on top of the mantle of hot magma underneath. Usually they move about as much as your fingernails grow in one year, which is only a couple of inches (cm), so we don't notice how slowly they creep. But over millions of years, they have moved apart enough to create seven continents, separated by oceans!

360 million years ago

55 million years ago

5 million years ago

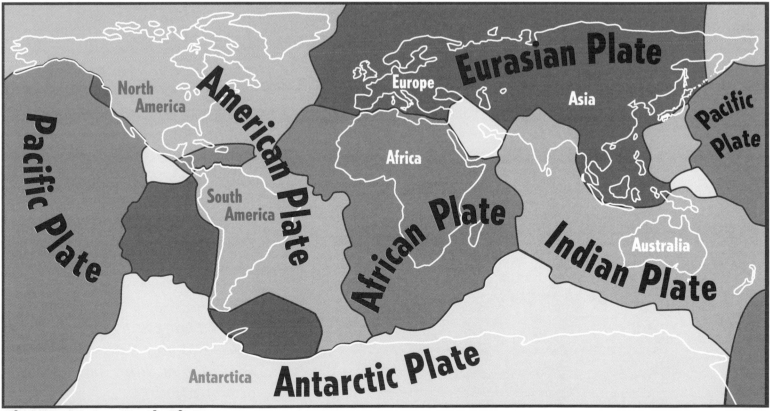

The Six Major Earth Plates

Push Those Plates!

A crack in the earth's crust is called a fault. *The large crack where two huge earth plates move against each other is called a* fault line. *Fault lines are where the action happens!*

You will need:
- Graham crackers
- Waxed paper spread with a thick layer of frosting or peanut butter

↻ Put two graham crackers very close to each other on the waxed paper and slowly push them apart. *You've made a* rift, *or big crack in the ocean floor. As the plates separate, magma oozes up from below and makes new ocean floor or creates underwater mountain ranges.*

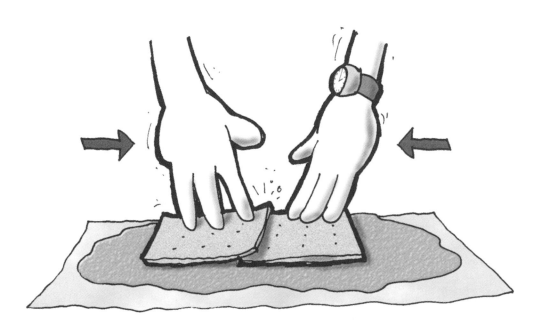

↻ Push two crackers toward each other, making one slide underneath the other. *When this happens on earth, watch out! The bottom plate starts to melt from the intense heat and pressure. It becomes new magma that floats up between the two plates, building up and up over many years until it finally causes a volcano blast! That plate action caused Mount Saint Helens in Washington State (page 16) to blow its top!*

⊘ **Put two graham crackers side by side on the waxed paper (wet the edge of one graham cracker first), and slowly push them together.** *The ridge of pushed-up cracker is just like many mountain ranges around the earth that were formed as two plates slowly crumpled together over millions of years. The Himalayas (the mountain range that includes Mount Everest) were formed when India "crashed" into Asia.*

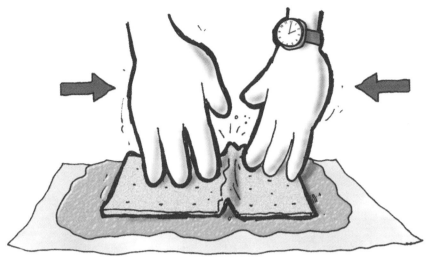

⊘ **Put two graham crackers side by side, and slide one up away from you and the other one down toward you.** *When plates move past each other like this, things don't exactly go smoothly. In fact, the plates usually get stuck on each other and then give a great lurch and move on, sending waves of vibrations through the earth's interior (much like the circular waves that ripple out when you drop a pebble in the water). These vibrations are so powerful that we have a special name for them — earthquake!*

Whose Fault Is This? What if you went outside after an earthquake and found the raspberries your family had planted in the front yard were now growing in front of your next-door neighbor's house (and in **your** yard were the roses from the next house)? This is what happened in San Francisco along one of the most famous fault lines in the world — the San Andreas Fault *in California, a 600-mile (950-km) boundary where the American and Pacific plates meet. In 1906, there was an earthquake along this fault line and the earth moved about 20 feet (6 m) in less than a minute! Wonder who got to eat the ripe berries?*

Measure a Quake Shake

Set up your equipment as shown on a table (a card table works well). Turn the dowel or rolling pin while a friend steadies the pen so it draws a straight line on the paper. Now, have the other friend sit facing the short end of the box and jiggle the table back and forth. How does the line change? Start a new straight line; then, have the friend shake the table as hard *as possible. How do your lines compare?*

You will need:
- Shoe box
- Scissors
- Wooden dowel or rolling pin
- Tape
- White paper
- Pen
- Two friends

One way geologists measure an earthquake is with an instrument called a

Modern seismograph

seismograph. This sensitive piece of equipment records vibrations in the earth, often

Ancient Chinese vase seismograph
(the balls dropped into the frogs' mouths when the earth shook)

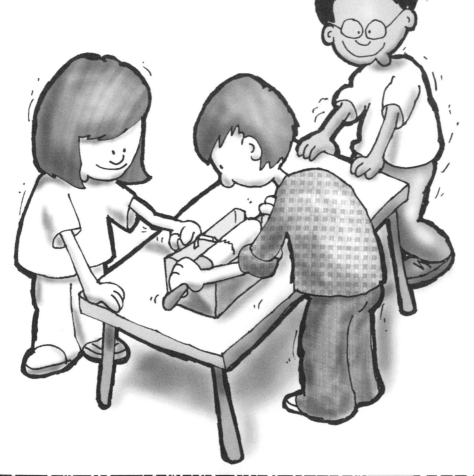

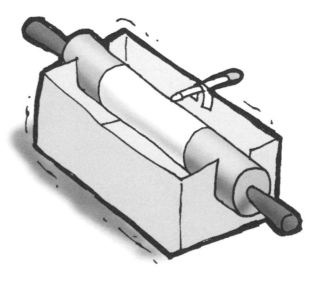

from thousands of miles (km) away, just as you recorded a the "quaking" table.

A *seismogram* (the printed record a seismograph produces) is a series of up-and-down marks measuring the amount of energy released by the quake. The larger "peaks" and "valleys" indicate the intense vibrations produced at the center of the quake.

Compare these two seismograms from actual earthquakes. Can you pick out the more powerful earthquake?

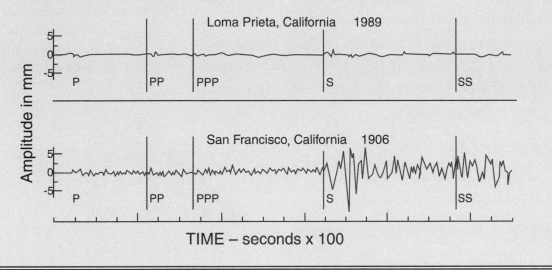

Inge Lehmann

Growing up in Denmark in the late 1800s, Inge Lehmann attended a school where boys and girls studied all the same subjects, and everyone played soccer and rugby and learned needlepoint! That style of education was unusual in those days.

After college, Lehmann went on to become the head of the seismology department of the Royal Danish Geodetic Institute. After years of studying seismograms, she proposed — and proved — that earth had an inner and outer core. Lehmann was a pioneer among women and scientists!

Do you think her early education, in which boys and girls were taught all the same subjects and participated in the same activities, had anything to do with her confidence in herself and what she achieved?

The Richter Scale

One of the ways that *seismologists* (size-MOL-oh-gists), geologists who study earthquakes, express the magnitude of an earthquake (the amount of energy released) is by using the *Richter* (RICK-ter) scale. On this scale, devised by American geologist Charles Richter, each level is *ten times* greater than the previous one! Turkey's earthquake of 1999 (one of the most destructive ever recorded) was just over 7.4 on the Richter scale.

Magnitude	What You Might See and Feel
1	Can only be detected by special instruments (Surprise! These mini-quakes occur about 8,000 times a day but you never feel them!)
5	Almost everyone feels this: most sleepers awakened; bells ring
6	Walls crack (Earthquakes of this magnitude or higher occur about once a year.)
8	Total destruction; the ground rises and falls in waves.

A Quake-Proof Contest!

The town of Quake, California, just suffered a serious earthquake. Before it rebuilds, a contest is being held to find someone who can design buildings that will withstand the next quake in Quake.

Gather a few friends, and see which of you would be hired to design buildings in this quake zone! Here are some options to get you started. To test your structures, build them on the washer — and then turn it on! May the best building win!

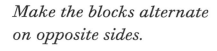

You will need:
- Building blocks
- Several bricks
- Box of sand
- Pieces of sponge, cut in squares and rectangles
- Paper-towel rolls
- Springs (optional)

Faulty Judgment?

An earthquake can kill or injure hundreds of people, and cleanup and repair of damaged structures costs millions of dollars. Should we restrict construction in earthquake-prone areas, like along the San Andreas Fault? Or do people have the right to build anywhere, regardless of safety concerns? Should cities spend money to protect people who knowingly build in dangerous areas? Should builders who build below-standard buildings be sued for damages after a quake?

Assembly

Make the pattern of the blocks identical on all sides.

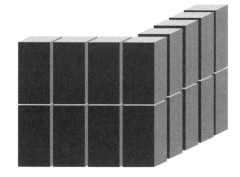

Make the blocks alternate on opposite sides.

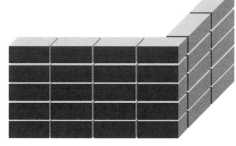

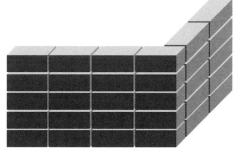

Place the longest side of the blocks lying down.

Place the longest side standing up.

Shape and Materials

Use pieces of sponge, or paper-towel rolls, rather than blocks. Compare buildings that are tall, short, or square.

Foundation

Try building on top of two bricks and on top of a box of sand. Or try building on springs. What's the sturdiest building you created? What was the weakest one?

BUILDING IT BETTER

Many people live near faults, prime earthquake territory. Most of the deaths and injuries during earthquakes are caused by damage to buildings, so designing structures that can withstand earthquakes is one of the most important things engineers, geologists, and architects can do to keep people in these areas safe. These scientists study buildings that have collapsed during quakes for clues as to how to make buildings stronger. To determine how manmade structures respond to tremors and quakes, organizations such as the USGS (United States Geological Survey) place special instruments in hospitals, bridges, dams, aqueducts, and highway overpasses to monitor the

Earthquake destruction • San Francisco, CA • 1989

motion. This information is used to develop requirements for where and how you can build in quake-prone areas.

Fido Knows

If your dog starts running around wildly, and barking or howling, he could be warning you that a quake is on the way! Earthworms crawl out of the ground and fish jump out of the water a few days before the earth starts rumbling. Although an animal's ability to "predict" an earthquake has never been scientifically proven, animal warnings of quakes have been recorded 2,500 years ago!

One explanation might be that some animals, like fish and earthworms, have finely tuned receptors that can detect subtle changes in the earth. A dog's more sensitive hearing probably helps him tell when small vibrations in the earth are increasing.

Quick Quake Check

The National Earthquake Information Center, based in Golden, Colorado, works with countries all over the world to gather information on earthquakes. You can check their Web site (wwwneic.cr.usgs.gov/neis) for a world map of recent earthquakes that's updated daily!

Quakes and Shakes

Those Earthly Gods!

In ancient Greece and Rome, people created stories called *myths* as explanations for the events of nature. The colorful characters in these stories were gods and goddesses, many of whom had earthly qualities.

The Romans told stories about Pluto, the god of the underworld. *Plutonic,* which means "rocks formed when magma cools deep within the earth," comes from his name. What word do you think came from Vulcan, a Roman god of fire who worked inside erupting mountains making weapons from lightning bolts?

Answer: Volcano!

Buildings crumbling and railroad tracks twisting aren't the only events that occur when the earth starts to shake. What else can happen when earth's plates bump together?

Look at this map of the world's earthquake zones next to this map of the world's active volcanoes. If you could put one map on top of the other, what would you notice about those two areas?

If you live in a part of the world where there are a lot of earthquakes, chances are excellent you're near some volcanoes, too! Most of the volcanoes in the world erupt where earth's plates are bumping together or moving apart.

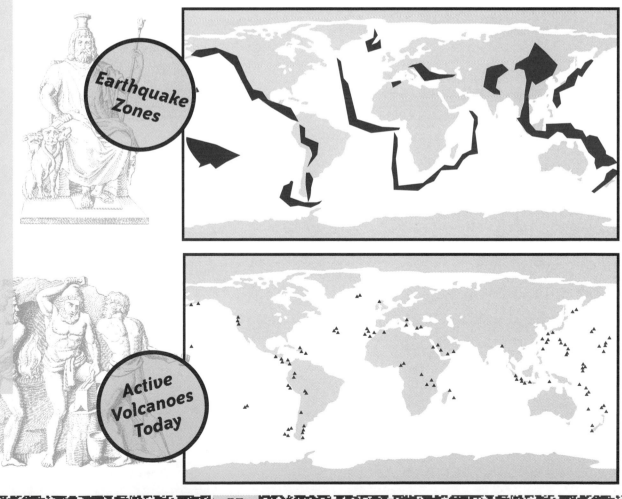

Earthquake Zones

Active Volcanoes Today

Thar She Blows!

Real volcano eruptions are pretty amazing (and scary!) to watch from a safe distance. But you can get right up close to a mini volcano in your backyard — and it's an awesome sight, too!

You will need:
- **Bottle with a narrow neck (a salad dressing bottle)**
- **Cake pan**
- **Soil or clay**
- **Funnel**
- **¼ cup (50 ml) baking soda**
- **Dish detergent**
- **¼ cup (50 ml) vinegar**
- **Red food coloring**

1. *Place the bottle in the middle of the cake pan. Mold soil or clay around it to make it look like a mountain.*

2. *Using the funnel, pour the baking soda into the bottle, and add a squirt of dish detergent.*

3. *Mix the vinegar with a few drops of the food coloring; then, pour it into the bottle. Watch as your mini Mount Saint Helens erupts!*

VOLCANOES AS EARTH *BUILDERS*

When a mountain blows its top, it sure is dramatic! But as you know, sometimes lava just flows out of a huge crack in the earth's surface or in the ocean floor. Is that still a volcano? You bet — and it also shapes the earth in dramatic ways. The *Columbia Plateau* (northwestern United States) is a good example. This *huge* section of flat rock formed when lava flowed through cracks in the earth's surface.

Look at all these important ways volcanoes are builders and shapers of land and life on our planet:

- *They add gases to the atmosphere.*

- *They add water to the oceans.*

- *They build chunks of continents, mountain ranges, and islands.*

- *Volcanic materials break down to make rich soil.*

- *Lava forms rocks.*

Manmade Volcanoes

Most movies about volcanoes blowing their tops are science fiction. How do moviemakers film those scenes? Producers use fog machines, burning gas lines, and other special effects to create a real-looking volcano on the set.

No Summer Vacation

In 1816, the people in the New England states, as well as in France, England, and Canada, were confused — and cold. It was summertime, so why was it snowing in June, with frost on the ground in July? The sky was hazy, and the sunsets were gorgeous. What was going on?

The year before, on a small island halfway around the world, the volcano Tambora had erupted, putting millions of tons of smoke and ash in the air. The smoke and ash traveled around the world on wind currents, blocking out the heat from the sun. The result? People in many northern parts of the world never got a summer!

In the Blink of an Eye

A family is sitting down to supper, laughing and chatting about the day's events. Suddenly, their house is completely filled with a flood of lava, preserving them just as they are, maybe in mid-sentence or even about to take a bite of food!

In the year 79 (almost 2,000 years ago), Mount Vesuvius in Italy erupted so quickly and unexpectedly that in less than a day, the entire town of nearby Pompeii was completely buried. We've learned much about this ancient culture from excavations of the town. Pompeii was the first site where scientists preserved their finds by making a plaster cast (page 80) of the imprints they left in the ash.

The Roman god Bacchus and Mount Vesuvius · detail from Roman fresco

I'm Cold! Turn Up the Volcano!

What's it like to live on top of a volcano? Ask the Icelanders!

The country of Iceland, an island in the North Atlantic, sits on one of the major fault lines, which is slowly pulling apart as the ocean widens. Lava flows up from below and hardens to fill the gap. Iceland has about 200 active volcanoes, many of which erupt frequently. The people in Iceland even pipe magma-heated water into their homes to keep them warm!

Huffing and Puffing in Hawaii

Mauna Loa in Hawaii is the world's largest active volcano. It starts out 15,000 feet (4,615 m) under the sea and goes up 13,784 feet (4,241 m) above sea level! Mauna Loa's explosions are still adding land to the island of Hawaii.

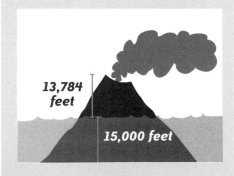

13,784 feet

15,000 feet

WATER, WATER EVERYWHERE!

What does water have to do with a book about geology? Well, for starters, the movement of water — from slow-moving rivers to pounding ocean waves to massive glaciers — is the *single largest force* shaping the surface of the earth. What's more, anywhere you dig into the crust of the earth, you'll eventually find water — a resource we depend on to survive. Learning about geology without exploring the wide world of water is like studying marine life and forgetting to talk about the ocean. So, let's dive in!

TAPPING INTO YOUR TAP WATER

Thirsty? Hands dirty? Turn on the tap and out flows clean water. In most areas of North America, we don't think about how far it has to travel to get to us and whether there will be enough of it. But in some parts of North America — and in most parts of the world — supplies of clean water are becoming harder to find.

__Try it!__ Ask a grown-up whether your home is on a public water system (your pipes connect to larger pipes owned by your town) or, *whether you have a private water supply, such as a well or cistern (a large tank) on your property.*

See if you can find the well, the cistern or the water meter. The natural source of water that supplies them might be many, many miles away!

Can you guess what determines how deep your well had to be, or how many miles of pipes the town water had to travel through to reach your house?

It's affected by soil, rocks, natural water sources ... in other words, geology!

I'm Soooo Thirsty!

About 97 percent of the earth's water supply is in the oceans. But we can't drink ocean water, of course, without taking the salt out first. How about the huge ice caps at the North and South Poles? They're all frozen solid.

That leaves less than 1 percent of the earth's water for us to drink. This drinking water includes our lakes, rivers, and streams, plus — one of our most important natural resources — our *groundwater*, the water that's always trickling among the rocks and through the cracks and spaces in them.

No matter where you are in the world — dry desert, frozen North Pole, on top of a mountain, or in your own backyard — if you dig deep enough, you'll hit water. Keep digging, and eventually, you'll get to an area that is always saturated (soaked) with water, called the *water table*. In the desert, you might have to dig hundreds of feet to reach it; in areas with a lot of rainfall, you probably have to go only a few feet.

Groundwater is the source of drinking water for more than half the people on earth!

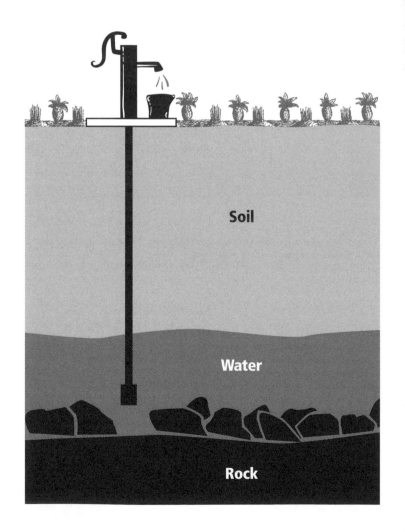

Soil

Water

Rock

A Hole in One!

You will need:
- Shovel
- Ruler
- Bucket of water
- Watch with second hand

Ask permission to dig a small hole in your backyard (promise to fill it in when you're finished). Dig it about 4 inches (10 cm) across and about 8 inches (20 cm) deep. Place a ruler in the hole and fill it with water. Time how long it takes for the water to drop 3 inches (8 cm). Does all the water drain out? Fill the hole again and time the water again. Is there a difference in the way the water drains the second time?

This simple test is called a *perc* (PERK) test. (Perc stands for *percolation*, which means liquid (in this case, water) seeping through solid materials, like soil.) Geologists and engineers do a series of perc tests just as you did to determine how fast water will move through the soil (the *perc rate*).

Water moves very quickly through sandy soil and more slowly through clay. What do you think, from your perc test, you have more of in your soil — sand or clay?

Generally, sandier soils are better locations for a house because they drain more quickly. Clay soils can have more potential for flooding after heavy rains.

A perc test also helps determine how water will flow from your natural water supply to your house, how you will get rid of your household wastewater, where your garden will grow best, and what kind of wildlife will be happy near your house. Wow! All that from digging a hole in the ground!

Pump Away!

Why is groundwater such a precious resource? Well, let's see what happens when we start pumping it out of the earth.

Put a 3-inch (7.5-cm) layer of gravel or stones in the container. Cover with a loose layer of soil. With the watering can, let it "rain" on your container until you have at least 2 inches (5 cm) of groundwater.

Let's say a family builds a house on this spot, and they need a well for drinking water. Stick a spray pump into the gravel and start pumping it (if the sprayer gets clogged, attach a small piece of a paper coffee filter to the open end with a rubber band). What happens to the level of the water in the container?

Now, a housing development goes in, so add three or four more pumps. It's a hot day and everyone in the neighborhood is running through the sprinklers or taking cool showers — have a friend help you spray all the pumps at once. How does the level of the groundwater change with more wells pumping water?

You will need:
- Gravel or aquarium stones
- Large rectangular clear plastic container
- Soil
- Watering can
- Clean spray pumps (from bottles of hand soap or glass cleaner)
- A friend

LOOSE SOIL

GRAVEL

3"

Every year there are *more people* on earth but the *same amount of water* for us to use.

Oops! Your next-door neighbor is changing the oil in his car, and he just spilled some of the old oil on the ground. Add a few drops of food coloring to the watering can, and water again. What effect does this polluted water have on your source of drinking water?

Whatever we spill on the earth could end up in the groundwater — water we have to drink!

Protect and Preserve!

One quart (1 L) of motor oil can pollute 250,000 gallons (1,000 L) of drinking water! You know other sources of groundwater pollution: septic systems that don't work properly, or landfills where the waste leaks into the ground. But what about some not-so-obvious pollutants like pesticides and fertilizers applied to farm crops? They, too, might find their way into the water supply.

Your actions can make a difference. Be careful about what you spill on the ground. Plus, take shorter showers, shut off the water while you brush your teeth, and keep a jug of chilled water in the fridge. They're all easy ways to preserve our drinking water.

Take Action for Water!

Adopt a pond or wetland. Have you been pestering your parents to get a dog or cat for a pet? Why not adopt a nearby natural resource instead? Your family can visit this new "family member" regularly to pick up trash and watch for any signs of pollution like a bad smell or a funny color. Fish and lots of small bugs are signs the water is healthy!

Form a partnership with a local water expert. Suggest to your teacher that your class participate in Give Water a Hand and work with natural resources experts to investigate and solve problems with the local water supply. Write or call: Give Water a Hand, University of Wisconsin, 1450 Linden Dr., 216 Agriculture Hall, Madison, WI 53706; 800-WATER-20.

HELP! IT'S RAINING POLLUTION!

In the 1980s, people began to notice that plant and animal life was declining or dying out completely. Scientists and ecologists figured out that a cycle of pollutants traveling from air to rain to soil was causing this change. Our cars and factories produce gases that end up in the air, making it dirty and sometimes unsafe to breathe. These chemicals then dissolve in rainwater, turning it into *acid rain*. When this rain falls back to earth, it destroys plants and animals that live in lakes and streams, kills entire forests, and affects our drinking water. Yikes!

An Acid Bath!

Acid rain wears away even the sturdiest stone buildings. The Parthenon in Athens, Greece, and the Great Sphinx in Egypt are two famous stone creations that are being badly damaged by acid rain. See acid rain in action for yourself.

With the paper clip, carve the chalk into a statue. Mix 1 tablespoon of water (15 ml) with the vinegar. This is your very strong acid rain. Use the medicine dropper to plop one drop of the mixture onto your statue, and closely watch the reaction. Predict what would happen if lots of acid rain fell for a long period of time.

You will need:
- **Paper clip**
- **Piece of real chalk (not gypsum chalk), available at most drugstores**
- **1 tablespoon (15 ml) vinegar**
- **Medicine dropper**

WATER POWER

It's easy to understand the force of water when we see pictures of tidal waves wiping out entire villages in coastal areas. And raging floods often destroy homes and properties that happen to be near an overflowing river.

But water usually works *much* more slowly and steadily as it shapes and reshapes the earth.

Rain, Rain, Flow Away

Place a bar of soap under the downspout of a gutter during a heavy rain. (Put rocks around the soap to hold it in place if you need to.) What happens to the soapsuds? Examine the bar of soap after the rainstorm. How has its shape been changed by the force of the rain?

Now, see how many areas you can find where this rain wore away the earth (the way it reshaped the bar of soap) or moved soil around (like the soapsuds). Check storm drains — what's piled up there? How about under your rain gutters? Look for signs of erosion at the bottom of steep hills or sloping driveways.

Rock Stars!

The Grand Canyon, Arizona

For millions of years, the Colorado River has carried crushed rock across a *plateau* (a broad, flat area) in northern Arizona, cutting deeper and deeper to form these high walls in beautiful hues of sandstone, limestone, and shale.

Wash & Wear!

Make a "mountain" of sand or soil at one end of a shallow baking pan. Tilt the mountain side as shown. Mark the edges of several Popsicle sticks every ¹/2 inch (1 cm) or so. Place these around the mountain, burying them at least 1¹/2 inches (3 cm). Cover the right side of the mountain with leaves and grass clippings.

Using a straw, try blowing away both sides of the mountain. Now, use a watering can to make it rain on the mountain. Judging from the marks on your sticks, which side is eroding more?

Erosion happens most quickly on bare sand, soil, or rocks. Wind, water, sun — even our footsteps! — can cause things to wear away. Whether we're talking about farm crops in a huge field, beach grass on the dunes, or the lawn in your backyard, plants do a super job of holding soil in place!

Should Nature Rule?

Ocean waves are constantly moving sand up and down the beach. Many beaches lose at least a foot (30 cm) of shoreline every year because of this erosion.

Many people want to preserve the beach. The solutions they propose are usually expensive and only temporary. Some say they cause *more* problems in the long run! Most geologists are in favor of letting nature take its course.

Should we spend millions of dollars to save the beaches? What do you think?

Ice Jam Ahead!

Frozen water is a force powerful enough to break apart even the biggest rocks, shaping mountains and valleys.

__Try it!__ Fill a glass bottle (one you don't want anymore) with very warm water. Put the cap on tightly. Put the bottle in a zippered freezer bag and then wrap it in several layers of newspaper; place the whole bundle in the freezer for two days. __With the help of an adult, and wearing work gloves__, carefully remove the package from the freezer and unwrap it. What has the change from hot to cold done to your bottle?

Cycles of hot sun and icy cold break apart even the strongest rocks. Water seeps into cracks in a rock, and if the temperature drops below the freezing point of 32 °F (0 °C), the water turns to ice. Ice takes up more space than liquid water, so as the water freezes, it pushes out the sides of the rock (or your bottle). As this cycle of freezing, thawing, and refreezing occurs over and over, the rock breaks apart.

Niagara Falls Is Falling!

The Niagara River flows north from Lake Erie to Lake Ontario, forming the boundary between the United States and Canada. Along the way, it plunges over one of the most famous waterfalls in the world, formed by a glacier about 10,000 years ago. When that huge torrent of water goes plummeting down, it digs what's called a *plunge pool* that undermines the cliffs, so they are literally falling into the river! As a result, Niagara Falls is actually 7 miles (11 km) farther upstream than it was when it was formed, and every year it's another 3 1/2 feet (1 m) closer to Lake Erie. But don't worry, at this rate, the falls will still fall for another 30,000 years!

Make a Mini Glacier

Pour a mixture of sand, gravel, and water into a milk carton, and put it in the freezer. When the mixture is solid, remove the carton. Go outside to a small hill — an area with soft soil and loose pebbles is perfect.

Starting at the top of the hill, push down on the ice block while you move it part of the way down the hill. Bear down hard, and see just how much you can change the way the earth looks.

Use sticks or string to mark where you started and stopped; then, do something else while you wait for the ice to melt. Come back and check out the result. What does the path of the glacier look like? What's left behind where the glacier melted?

During the most recent Ice Age (10,000 years ago), the temperature on earth got much colder for many years in a row. Huge piles of ice called *glaciers* built up at the North Pole, and then started to move south. At one time, they covered most of Canada and spread into the United States. As the glaciers moved along, they picked up huge rocks, shaped mountains, and carved valleys. When the earth warmed up again, the ice melted, leaving piles of ground-up rocks and lakes behind.

Rock Stars!

The Old Man of the Mountain, New Hampshire

This "Great Stone Face" of granite was formed entirely by melted water from a glacier freezing and thawing in the rock crevices.

CAN WE STILL SEE GLACIERS?

Sure! Although the weather is not cold enough right now for glaciers to cover most of the world, there are a few places in the world (high mountains and countries near the North and South Poles) where you can go to see glaciers. One place is Glacier National Park, way up in the Rocky Mountains in Montana. This beautiful park is open for only a few months each summer — the rest of the time there is too much snow on the ground for people to get in! If you go, make sure you take a coat and camera — so you can get a picture of you making a glacier snowman in July!

Ahern and Old Sun Glaciers • Glacier National Park, Montana

Don't Hide Under this Haystack!

Have you ever come across a very large rock just sitting all by itself on top of the ground in the middle of an open area? These rocks, called haystacks, *are common in New England and across the northern prairies. A glacier may have carried them more than 1,000 miles (1,600 km) before depositing them!*

Rock Stars!

The Matterhorn, Zermatt, Switzerland
When two glaciers crept down from the north, they broke off huge chunks of this mountain, creating its famous sharp steep peak.

ROCK RECORDINGS

**Touch the earth and listen to the rocks
for they remember
They know and remember
all that has come to pass here.**
—*Lee Henderson*

Do you like to look at photographs of yourself taken when you were younger? Going through photo albums and scrapbooks is a great way to get a glimpse of someone's past. And, in a way, that's exactly what geologists do to learn about earth's history. The earth is like a big scrapbook with fossil "photographs" and other clues about the past 4½ billion years of life pressed into its rock "pages." But just as a collection of photos and mementos from a person's life doesn't tell you everything (or might not be all in one place), scientists have to piece together the earth's past from the fossils and other artifacts, filling in the history as they gather new finds. You can "read" the earth's history all around you, too — and begin drawing your own conclusions!

FIGURING OUT FOSSILS

If you found the imprint of a plant or animal pressed into a rock, what would be your first guess about your discovery? When humans first began finding this evidence of past life, they had never seen anything like it, so they interpreted it in terms of what they knew about earth and what was important in their lives. Here are some beliefs about early fossil findings for you to chuckle over!

Today, we understand that fossils are the preserved remains of plants and animals, and what's more, we know fossils give us the best clues about earth's past. We are still searching for clues to answer the question "What was the earth like millions of years ago?" Are you ready to help?

● **bones of monsters, or weapons the gods had tossed down after a fight**
(Native American explanation for petrified tree trunks)

● **devil's toenails**
(a large claw-shaped shell found in Europe)

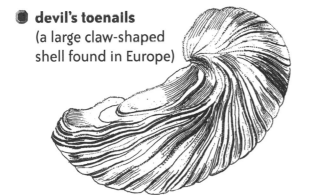

● **magical snake eggs**
(small, round sea urchins)

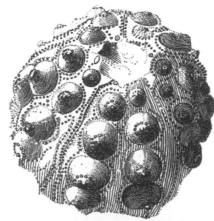

● **objects that grew within the earth because of mystical currents that traveled through the rocks**
(explanation of fossils popular during the Middle Ages)

Language Links

Paleontology (pay-lee-an-TOL-oh-jee) has Greek roots: *pale* (long ago) + *onta* (existing things) + *ology* (the study of), or "the study of life that existed long ago." A *paleontologist* is a scientist who studies fossil remains of plants and animals and how they relate to the history of the earth.

Find the Fossil Fakes!

Four of these items are usually defined as fossils. Can you pick them?

Mummy	**Arrowhead**	**Leaf print in stone**
Frozen mammoth	**Piece of coral**	**Stone tablet with writing**
Cave painting	**Dinosaur bone**	**Piece of old pottery**
Pyramids of Egypt	**Petrified tree**	**Handprint in concrete**

A fossil is the remains, impression, or trace of an animal or plant that lived long ago and is no longer around. It can be the actual organism as well as its tracks, droppings, or eggs. So, if the plant or animal is still around today, some scientists would argue that any preserved sign you might find of it is technically not a fossil.

HOW IMPRESSIVE!

Most fossils are created when an impression of something that was once alive is captured in rock. Use your geology skills to guess which type of rock forms the most fossils. Here's the fossil-forming process to give you some clues:

1.

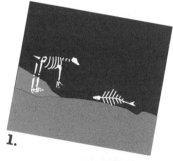
2.

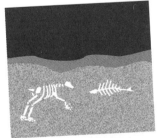

3.

4.

1. The plant or animal dies and the soft parts rot away, leaving hard parts like bones or teeth.

2. The remains are buried in sediment in a wet place, like the muddy bottom of a lake.

3. Water and dissolved minerals slowly replace the original materials that made up the plant or animal.

4. Pressure from more layers of sediment gradually turn the water/mineral solution to stone.

Answer: sedimentary rock

Great Geologists!

Mary Anning

"She sells seashells by the seashore." You've probably tried to say that three times fast! Mary Anning, who inspired that tongue twister, grew up in the early 1800s on the coast of England. She noticed that fossil collectors were selling fossil shells for high prices, so she began collecting shells to sell in her father's souvenir shop.

Mary was only 12 when she discovered her first skeleton (a dolphinlike reptile called an ichthyosaur). The skeletons of prehistoric marine fossils that Mary Anning found are now on display in museums all over the world!

Turn That Bone to Stone!

Cut two pieces of sponge into bone shapes. Set one piece aside for comparison. Fill a cup with hot water. Stir in Epsom salts until no more will dissolve. Add a few drops of food coloring; then pour this mixture into the pan.

Put one sponge bone into the pan and watch the water travel through the holes. Set the pan in a place where it won't be disturbed for several days. When the sponge is completely dry, feel it. Is it harder or softer than the comparison piece? Look carefully in the holes. What do you see?

All living things have holes in them. (You sweat through holes in your skin.) *Petrified fossils* are made when water that has lots of minerals in it seeps into the holes found in natural items (like bones, plant parts, or seashells, for example). The minerals cling to the sides of the holes. When the water dries up, the minerals crystallize (page 36) in the holes, replacing the original material that may have rotted away. The minerals in the Epsom salts formed crystals, petrifying your sponge "bone"!

You will need:
- 🪨 **Scissors**
- 🪨 **An old sponge**
- 🪨 **A cup and a shallow pan**
- 🪨 **Epsom salts (available at a drugstore)**
- 🪨 **Food coloring**

I'm Petrified!

The English word *petrify* comes from the Latin word *petra*, which means "rock" or "stone." Have you ever awakened from a bad dream and been so scared you couldn't even reach out to turn on the light? When you're so frightened that you can't move — as if you've turned to stone — you're petrified!

A Paleontologist's Puzzle

Test your friends to see how good they would be on a fossil dig! Place 10 Popsicle sticks side by side and tape them together on only one side. Draw a picture of your favorite dinosaur on the other side. Take the tape off and mix the sticks together. Give the puzzle to a friend and ask him or her to put it together without knowing what the picture is! To make it even harder (and more like a real paleontologist's job), remove five sticks from the puzzle before you give it to your friend.

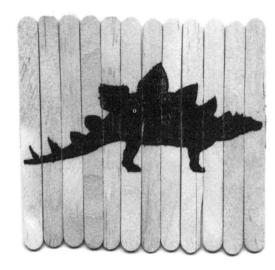

THEY CAN DO IT!

As amazing as it sounds, paleontologists can reconstruct entire animals from one small fossilized piece (many early species of sharks were reconstructed from just one tooth fossil!). When paleontologists find a fragment of a tooth, bone, or shell, they first identify the type of animal (usually not too difficult, because types of animals can be grouped by distinctive features of these fragments). Then, they reconstruct the skeleton, using its close relatives as a guide. Once the skeleton is complete, it's not hard to fill in the muscles that give the animal its shape and posture. Lastly, the scientists make some guesses as to skin and color.

The result? The model of the *Stegosaurus* that you view in amazement at your favorite natural history museum!

The Misnamed Dino

Sometimes paleontologists do put skeletons together incorrectly. In 1879, famous fossil hunter O.C. Marsh found parts of a huge skeleton in Wyoming. He was in a big hurry to put it together and name it before his rival, Edward Drinker Cope, found out. But it was missing a lot of pieces, including the skull. Marsh drew a picture of the complete skeleton, adding a head found not very far away that looked as if it would fit with the body. He then named this new dinosaur *Brontosaurus*.

About 25 years later, another paleontologist showed that the *Brontosaurus* was actually the same species of dinosaur as the *Apatosaurus*, which Marsh had discovered and named two years earlier! Many people still incorrectly refer to the *Apatosaurus* as *Brontosaurus*. Then, in the 1970s, paleontologist Jack McIntosh realized that Marsh had used the head of the *Camarasaurus*! This mistake has been corrected, but for about 100 years, models were shown in museums with the wrong head! (There is no dinosaur called *Brontosaurus*.)

The Fudge Factor

Competing against others can make you focus your efforts and try harder to succeed, whether it's in a soccer game or on a spelling test. With everyone striving for the same goal, you invest more of yourself so you can achieve the results you want.

But sometimes the desire to win overcomes good judgment, so people "fudge" facts or bend the rules to be the winner. Scientists compete with each other to be the first to find a cure or to make an incredible discovery. Have you ever "stretched the truth" a bit to get recognition? How did you feel about it afterward?

Rock Stars!

Dinosaur National Monument, Utah
Watch paleontologists chip away at this ridge of sandstone full of fossils at the Dinosaur Quarry Visitor's Center!

Great Geologists!

Christopher Wolfe

"I thought I'd faint," is how Christopher Wolfe described the way he felt when, at age 7, he found a dinosaur bone while fossil hunting in 1996 near the Arizona–New Mexico border with his parents. Christopher's dad, a paleontologist, found more dinosaur bones. They had stumbled upon an unknown species of a horned dinosaur that was 20 million years older than any horned dinosaur previously found in North America. And Christopher really made a name for himself with his find — his dad named the new species Zuniceratops christopheri.

A Fossil Hunt!

So, where are the best places to look for fossils? Anywhere you find sedimentary rock (page 23) for starters! That means stream banks, shorelines, riverbanks and other places where sediment is piling up.

Digging exposes rock that has been protected (in fact, geologists find most fossils by breaking open rocks to reveal older layers). So, try fossil hunting in areas where excavating is being done — where a new road is being cut through rock, for example.

Sticky Situations

If you saw the movie *Jurassic Park*, then you already know one of the other ways that an animal can become fossilized: It can get trapped in amber (sticky tree sap). The sap hardens, and the specimen (usually an insect) is perfectly preserved.

But what would happen to a prehistoric saber-toothed cat heading for water, crossing a section of the earth that's sticky with tar? Uh-oh! It's stuck fast! Thousands of years ago, scores of unlucky animals were trapped in tar that had oozed up from deep in the ground at the La Brea Tar Pits in the middle of what is now Los Angeles, California. They eventually became buried in layers of sediment, creating perfectly preserved fossils that modern-day paleontologists uncovered!

Life-size replicas of mammoths near a tar pool
• La Brea Tar Pits • Los Angeles, California

Think About It!

Brr..!

THE BIG CHILL

Occasionally, in climates where the soil remains permanently frozen, entire bodies of ancient animals have remained frozen solid — thousands of years after they died! The remains of frozen woolly mammoths and woolly rhinoceros date back 10,000 years, to the last Ice Age!

A Frozen Fossil?

Or should we call it something else? Scientists disagree over whether these frozen specimens or those preserved in sap have actually been fossilized, because none of the original material of the animal has been replaced. What would *you* call them?

Make a Good Impression!

When a leaf, shell, or footprint leaves a mark, or impression, in soft mud, and the mud hardens to rock before the impression gets washed away or erased, the fossil made is called a mold. *Sometimes the hard mold gets filled with another material, like sand or clay, that also hardens to rock, forming a* cast. *It's easy to make your own mold and cast collection!*

You will need:
- 🐚 3 cups (750 ml) plaster of paris (available at a hardware store)
- 🐚 Plastic ziplock bag
- 🐚 Aluminum pie plate
- 🐚 Petroleum jelly
- 🐚 Sand
- 🐚 Food coloring

To make a mold:

Pour the plaster and 1 cup (250 ml) of water into the bag. Carefully squeeze the mixture until all the lumps are gone and it looks like thick cake batter. Pour it into the pie plate.

Press your hand firmly into the plaster to make a good impression. (If there isn't a clear imprint, smooth it out, let the plaster set for a minute, then press your hand in again.) Wait a few hours until the plaster is very dry.

***Note:** Never flush or pour plaster down a drain. Discard in trash only.*

To make a cast:

After the mold has dried, smear petroleum jelly over the whole mold (this makes the cast easier to remove). Mix together another batch of plaster, this time adding some sand and food coloring.

Pour the mixture over your mold and let it dry completely (it'll take a few hours). Use a thin nail to carefully pry around the edges and separate your cast and mold.

Strut Your Stuff!

Fossil footprints, especially several in a row, give paleontologists a lot of information about an extinct animal. To see how this works, you'll need a kid who's much younger than you, an adult, and yourself!

First, measure a distance of 30 feet (9 m) and mark each end with a piece of string. Start with your right toes on the string and take a step with your left foot. Counting every time you put your right *foot down, record the number of steps taken. Now, count the number of steps the smaller kid and the adult take to cover this distance. Then, record the number of steps each person takes to cover this distance when running.*

Let's say you're a paleontologist and you've just found a trackway, *or path of fossil footprints, showing these different strides. What could you learn about the three "animals"?*

The following questions may help you draw some conclusions: Who takes more steps to cover the distance — the tallest or the shortest person? Why? Do you take more steps to cover the distance when you're running or walking?

By measuring the *size* of the footprints and

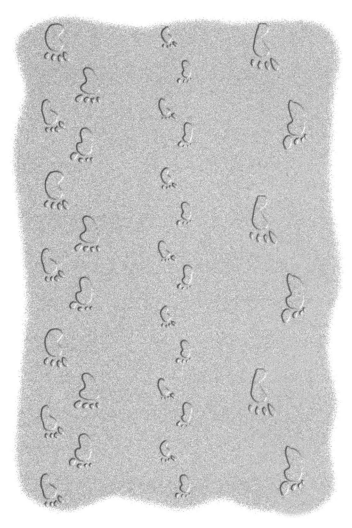

how far apart they are, the scientists can estimate the size of the animal, whether it walked on two feet or four, if it was running or moving slowly, if it liked to be alone or in a big group, and more!

Cast of Thousands

Complete fossil skeletons are hard to find, and expensive to buy, so museums use the mold and cast method to make copies. Then, they sell them to other museums. Many dinosaur skeletons you see are well-made plaster casts of the real thing.

Great Geologists!

Charles Lydell

In the early 1800s, the Scottish scientist Charles Lydell was the first person to express the age of the earth in millions of years.

He proposed that the geological events of long ago had occurred at the same rate as the ones we see happening around us today — very slowly.

His ideas helped people understand the huge amounts of time that geology encompasses.

Long, Long, Ago . . .

Being a geologist means trying to understand huge amounts of time that are almost impossible to imagine. Here's a way to help you picture them.

You'll need a carton of table salt and measuring spoons and cups. Imagine that each grain of salt represents one year. Count out as many grains as you are years old.

Now, someone, believe it or not, took the time to count how many grains of salt there are in 1 teaspoon (5 ml). Whew! Aren't you glad that wasn't your math homework? It turns out there are about 100,000 grains (or years)!

Measure 3 teaspoons (15 ml) of salt. You're looking at about 300,000 years. That's when the first modern humans appeared on earth.

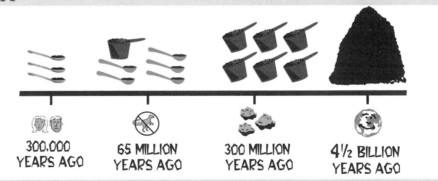

300,000 YEARS AGO   65 MILLION YEARS AGO   300 MILLION YEARS AGO   4½ BILLION YEARS AGO

Now measure 1 cup plus 5 tablespoons (265 ml) of salt. That represents 65 million years ago, when dinosaurs became extinct.

Picture 6 cups (1.5 L) of salt. That's when coal began to form 300 million years ago.

The oldest rocks we've found on earth so far formed about 3.9 billion years ago — that's more than 81 (20 L) cups of salt!

And, are you ready for this? The earth formed 96 cups (24 L), or 4½ billion grain-years, of salt ago!

EARTH-MADE ENERGY

What if we could lock away the tremendous energy of the sun inside the earth to use for power many, many years later? Sounds like a great idea, doesn't it? Well, surprise! The earth already did it for us millions of years ago. You use it every day! When you ride on the school bus, heat your home, and cook your food, you're using *fossil fuels* like coal or oil, sources of energy made from the remains of once-living organisms.

A Mini Coal Mine

It's hard to believe, looking at a hard, shiny, black lump of coal, that it's a nugget of stored plant energy!

Here's a way to see the beginnings of how coal is made deep inside the earth. With a grown-up's help, cut a 2-quart (2-L) soda bottle just below the shoulder. Fill the bottle with plant materials like leaves and grass clippings. Cover with water. Press a plastic lid, rim side up, down on the plants and weight it with rocks. Use the cut-off top to make a seal that will help keep out the air. Put the bottle in a warm place and push down on the sliding seal every day. Watch as your plant parts get compacted together.

As prehistoric plants fell to the ground, sometimes they were buried by layers of other plants. Without air, they didn't decompose. As more and more plants fell down, the ones on the bottom were heating up and getting compressed. Over millions of years, as the water was squeezed out, this plant material became coal!

Fill It with Ferns, Please!

Think About It!

You're sitting in the car at the gas station. Hear those million-year-old plants and animals flowing into your tank?

Gasoline, the fuel that most of our cars run on, comes from *petroleum*, formed when layers of plants and animals were buried under mud on the ocean floor. Over millions of years, these remains were transformed into a sticky, black substance. Petroleum slowly flows through porous (has lots of air spaces) rocks like sandstone, but it collects in large underground pools (reservoirs), when it reaches layers of rocks it can't move through. We pump petroleum out of the ground and process it into everything from lip balm to plastic bags to road tar.

When you turn up the oil- or gas-burning furnace in your house, put your sandwich in a plastic bag, or drive on a paved road, you're using petroleum products.

Saving Up!

Coal, gasoline, and other fossil fuels are what we call *nonrenewable resources* — they aren't replacing themselves as quickly as we are using them up. What can *you* do about it? Talk with your family and friends about ways we can save our fossil fuels.

REGULAR FERN | EXTRA FERN | SUPER FERN

STONE, SWEET HOME

We collect rocks, we *ooh* and *aah* over awesome rock formations in the landscape, and — if you look around — you'll notice that a lot of us live in rocks, too! Early humans quickly figured out that natural rock formations like caves made sturdy shelters; then, they stacked rocks together to make homes. Where rocks aren't available, we've figured out how to make our own! Come explore the world of caves and other stone structures.

Candy Caves

Stack some sugar cubes against the side of a glass. Put a thin layer of clay over the top of the sugar cubes. Using a toothpick, poke a few holes in the clay. Now, use a spray bottle or eye-dropper to make it "rain." What happens as the water gets into the cracks and collects at the bottom?

← CLAY

← SUGAR

FROM CRACKS TO CAVES

Most caves form when water that has a little bit of acid in it seeps down through the soil (your clay) until it hits limestone (your sugar cubes). The water seeps into tiny cracks in the rock and starts to dissolve it, bit by bit. A long time goes by; more and more water gets into the cracks, and more and more limestone erodes. After hundreds of thousands of years, when the cracks in the rocks are so big that we can walk right into them, they're called caves!

Blackgang cave • Isle of Wight, England

Language Links

The Latin word *cavus*, which means "hollow," is the root of our words *cave* — and *cavity*. When you think about it, your mouth is a bit like a cave itself. It is dark and wet (but much hotter than most underground caves). And mini caves can even form in the "rocks" you use for chewing. When the bacteria in your saliva break down sugars in the food you eat, a mild acid is produced. When there is too much acid in your mouth (that doesn't get brushed away), it can eat small holes, or cavities, in your teeth. That's when you visit the dentist to get your "mouth caves" filled.

Cave-cicles

As the limestone dissolves, it creates calcite crystals in two formations:

• *stalactites,* which hang from the ceiling of the cave (think "t" as in "from the **t**op")

• *stalagmites,* which grow from the floor of the cave and point up (think "g" as in "from the **g**round").

In nature, it takes millions of years for these cave-cicles to grow even an inch. But there's a much faster way to make your own!

Pour hot water into the cups. Stir in Epsom salts until no more will dissolve.

Soak the string in one cup; then, tie a nail at each end of the string. Place the two cups at opposite ends of a piece of cardboard. Put one nail into each cup, carefully making a small dip in the middle of the string. Keep this experiment in a place where it will not be disturbed. Check on it every day, and watch as your cave-cicles get larger.

You will need:
- 2 cups
- Epsom salts (available at a drugstore)
- Cotton or wool string
- 2 nails
- Cardboard

Rock Stars!

Mammoth Cave National Park, Kentucky
The world's largest cave system has 150 miles (250 km) of passageways, and even an underground sea!

UNDERGROUND HONEYCOMBS

Before there were cemeteries, people would bury their dead in caves. A really important person might have a cave all to him or herself, but many times the cave was shared by a whole family. In ancient Rome, there was a whole system of manmade underground burial caves called *catacombs*, with tunnel-like hallways that went from cave to cave.

The catacombs of San Marcellino near Rome, Italy

ROCK BUILDING-BLOCKS

In some areas of the world, there isn't a lot of rock available for building materials. But humans have been very inventive at combining materials at hand to create rock-like mixtures to build with. Clay, soil, straw, crushed-up limestone, shale, gravel, and water are all ingredients used to make bricks, cement, and concrete — the materials we use to build houses, sidewalks, streets, and skyscrapers.

Language Links

Concrete or Cement?

Cement (mostly powdered clay and limestone) is the glue that holds water, sand, and gravel together to make *concrete*, a sturdy building material. Here are two ways to help you remember the difference between these two words. You might suggest to a friend that you *cement* an agreement you just made (glue it together) by sharing an ice cream cone. The date for your sleepover party next week is set in *concrete* (it's firm and it won't change).

Bake a Brick!

In some hot, dry areas around the world, people mix mud and water together and let it bake in the sun to make a type of brick called *adobe*, which means "clay" in Spanish.

Try it! To make your own adobe bricks, mix about 2 cups (500 ml) of soil (a clay soil is best) with dry grass clippings or straw. Then, add just enough water to make a really stiff mud that's hard to stir. Pour this mixture into an ice cube tray, and set it in the sun to dry. After about 10 days, pop out a mini brick and drop it. (If it breaks, the adobe isn't dry yet.) Let it dry a few more days. When it doesn't break when dropped, you have adobe bricks ready for building! Mix up a fresh batch of mud to hold your bricks together.

Think About It!

Smart Choices!

If brick and stone houses are the sturdiest places in which to live, why doesn't everyone build one? What makes sense to use as a building material depends mainly on where you live. In areas of North America with plenty of forests, wooden houses are quite common. In Mexico and parts of the southwestern United States, where the landscape is desert, adobe is the building material of choice.

What are most of the houses in your neighborhood made of? What does that tell you about the availability of building materials near you?

Can You Straighten the Leaning Tower?

The Leaning Tower of Pisa

Sometimes, using the sturdiest building materials you can find isn't good enough, if you're not careful where you put them!

In 1174, Bonnano Pisano, an Italian engineer, started building a seven-level bell tower in Pisa, Italy, to complete the city's cathedral. After he built three stories of white marble on a foundation of stone, he noticed the tower was leaning! The soil underneath it was too soft, and the bell tower was sinking on one side! Over the next 200 years, different things were tried to finish the Leaning Tower of Pisa, as it came to be called, and make it straight again.

Today, the top edge is more than 17 feet (5 m) away from where it should be — and still tilting! This world-famous tourist attraction has been closed to the public since 1990 for safety reasons.

Here's what's been done to the tower so far in a series of attempts to straighten it:

• Marble was added on the low side of the first three levels to even things out. But that only made matters worse!

• In 1275, three more levels were added that hung out over the edge of the high side. That didn't work either.

• In 1934, the government tried to pump concrete under the tower to push it back up. Still no success.

• But in the spring of 1999, the lean of the tower was corrected by $1/5$ of an inch (4 mm)! That may not seem like much, but the experts involved in the experiment said it exceeded their expectations! Brainstorm with a friend to see if you can figure out what they might have done.

Answer: Workers removed soil from under the tower's base, allowing the tower to settle more securely into the ground. Two sets of steel suspenders, anchored to giant cranks in the ground, were attached to the tower, ready to tighten just in case the digging made the tower wobble!

HELP! MY HOUSE IS DROWNING!

In some areas of the world, people have tried to make more land to live on by filling in shallow, swampy areas with soil. In Amsterdam and San Francisco, people have piled tons of dirt in the water, then built buildings on top. But just as with the Leaning Tower of Pisa, the soil isn't strong enough to hold the weight. Some houses have sunk so much that their garage doors are halfway underground!

The people in these areas could have learned a lot by talking to folks in places like New Orleans, Louisiana, and Rotorua, New Zealand. The water table (page 62) is so high in those parts of the world that these people live literally just above water. It's impossible for them to dig basements under their houses — they would fill right up with water. And people in these areas cannot be buried underground. Instead, special tombs, called *mausoleums*, are built above ground.

Rock Stars!

Mesa Verde National Park, Colorado

After this sandstone plateau eroded to form steep canyons riddled with caves, a prehistoric people called the Anasazi filled the caves with an amazing series of cliff dwellings made from adobe. For some reason, about 700 years ago, the Anasazi left this area, but the ruins are still there.

ROCK ON!

Well, now you've got an awesome rock collection (and maybe a coin collection, too), you're an expert on the best fossil-hunting spots, you've exploded a volcano, created a cave, sculpted in sandstone and watched acid rain at work. Wow! You're an earth expert! Why not celebrate with your friends by hosting a special Geology Rocks party! Here are some ideas to get you started!

> ~
> For a real "rock"-ing time, come to my house next Saturday at 3 PM. Please bring something to add to our pot of Stone Soup.

Stone Soup

Scrub a smooth, hand-sized stone until it is very clean. Put it in a large pot of water with some salt and pepper. As your guests arrive, add each of their ingredients to the soup (pasta, beans, veggies, and canned tomatoes are all good additions). Bring to a boil; then, simmer over medium heat for about 1 hour.

While the soup is cooking, play geology games, make crafts, and have a treasure hunt. You might want to include the following:

> **Earth-Treasures Scavenger Hunt (page 14)**
> **Sand sculptures (page 25)**
> **Mancala (page 37)**
> **Micro-meteorite collectors (page 43)**

While you're rockin' on, you'll want to rock out, too! So tune in to your favorite rock station! Then, top off the party with dessert — marble cake, of course!

•

Create Invitations on Marbled Paper

•

**Serve:
Stone Soup
Marble Cake
Fudge Ripple
Ice Cream**

•

Have Fun!

RESOURCES

Allison, Linda. *The Reason for Seasons.* Yolla Bolly Press (Little, Brown & Company), 1975.

Allison, Linda. *The Wild Inside.* Yolla Bolly Press (Little, Brown & Company), 1988.

Anderson, Alan, Gwen Diehn, and Terry Krautwurst. *Geology Crafts for Kids.* Sterling Publishing, 1996.

Bramveil, Martyn. *Understanding and Collecting Rocks and Fossils.* Usborne Publishing, 1983.

Lambert, David. *Rocks and Minerals.* Franklin Watts, 1986.

Lawton, Rebecca, Diana Lawton, and Susan Panttaja. *Discover Nature in the Rocks: Things to Know and Things to Do.* Stackpole Books, 1997.

Leavitt, Duane L., ed. *Activities and Resources for Earth Science Teachers* (The CREST Project/ The National Science Foundation). Maine Geological Survey, 1991.

Niles, Gregory and Douglas Eldredge. *The Fossil Factory: A Kid's Guide To Digging Up Dinosaurs, Exploring Evolution and Finding Fossils.* Addison-Wesley, 1989.

Parker, Steve. *Eyewitness Explorers: Rocks and Minerals.* Dorling Kindersley, 1993.

Ranger Rick's Nature Scope. *Geology: The Active Earth.* McGraw-Hill, 1997.

Smith, Bruce and David McKay. *Geology Projects for Young Scientists.* Franklin Watts, 1992.

Thompson, Sharon Elaine. *Death Trap: The Story of the La Brea Tar Pits.* Lerner Publications, 1995.

INDEX

More Good Books from Williamson Books

Williamson Books are available from your bookseller or directly from Ideals Publications

KALEIDOSCOPE KIDS® Books
Where Learning Meets Life!

THE LEWIS & CLARK EXPEDITION
The Untold Stories
by Carol A. Johmann

ANCIENT ROME!
Exploring the Culture, People & Ideas
of This Powerful Empire
by Avery Hart and Sandra Gallagher

SKYSCRAPERS!
Super Structures to Design & Build
by Carol A. Johmann

Children's Book Council Notable Book
American Bookseller Pick of the Lists
KNIGHTS & CASTLES
50 Hands-On Activities to Experience the
Middle Ages
by Avery Hart and Paul Mantell

American Bookseller Pick of the Lists
Parent's Guide Children's Media Award
ANCIENT GREECE!
40 Hands-On Activities to Experience
This Wondrous Age
by Avery Hart and Paul Mantell

Benjamin Franklin Silver Award
GOING WEST!
Journey on a Wagon Train to Settle a
Frontier Town
by Carol A. Johmann and Elizabeth J. Rieth

Parents' Choice Recommended
BRIDGES!
Amazing Structures to Design, Build & Test
by Carol A. Johmann and Elizabeth J. Rieth

To see what's new with Williamson Books and Ideals Publications and learn more about specific titles, visit our website at:
www.idealsbooks.com

To Order Books:

You'll find Williamson Books at your favorite bookstore, or you can order directly from Ideals Publications. We accept Visa and MasterCard (please include the number and expiration date).

Order on our secure website:
www.idealsbooks.com

Toll-free phone orders with credit cards:
1-800-586-2572

Toll-free fax orders:
1-888-815-2759

Or send a check with your order to:
Ideals Publications
Williamson Books Orders
2630 Elm Hill Pike, Suite 100
Nashville, Tennessee 37214

Catalog request: web, mail, or phone

Please add $4.00 for postage for one book plus $1.00 for each additional book. Satisfaction is guaranteed or full refund without questions or quibbles.